Welcome!
What's the F-U-N way to learn?

 **F** FIND YOUR TYPE

 **U** UNDERSTAND YOURSELF

 **N** NEXT STEPS FOR GROWTH

A powerful tool for self-discovery, the FUNeagram™ is a creative, welcoming, and simplified way to use the Enneagram's basic principles.

THE FUN WAY TO LEARN THE ENNEAGRAM

FUNEAGRAM™

www.FUNeagram.com

Preface

Why I created FUNeagram™ and wrote this workbook.

I love the Enneagram because it is a journey, not a destination. It's an ongoing experience, and a forever path of learning. I have worked with it over 25 years and continue to learn and grow. I see the Enneagram as a map to empowerment containing silver linings, along with great support for both embracing strengths and facing shadows.

Finding your type is the first part of the journey. The next part is the evolution of growth and self-discovery for your whole lifetime. I created FUNeagram™ because I wanted to offer a different approach to this exploration. I was inspired to see how the Enneagram was organized based on the ancient diagram. I was fascinated to see how the complex parts go much deeper than the nine numbers.

My idea was to highlight the organizing elements and use them to create a new way to learn the Enneagram. Almost like a new doorway or approach that is different from a test or a book. *And why not make it FUN!?*

This journey is like a river flowing forward through ever-changing landscapes. You are in your own boat, and you are navigating and experiencing the river as you go. You can row along and be suddenly surprised by jagged rocks or challenging rapids, or even coming into stagnant waters. And then the weather changes. And you turn out to be stronger than you thought. Or not at all what you thought. And this is only the beginning of your ride on the river—your bigger life journey.

Why the illustrious river analogy? Discovering yourself through the Enneagram is alot like that. Everyone has their own way of learning about the Enneagram. How you find your type is absolutely a valuable part of the whole experience. **Maybe you land on one type and later find out you relate more to another type on a deeper and more true level.** Maybe you spend months or years looking at yourself through one type and one day you row around the bend and discover you really aren't that type at all, and you enjoy exploring this new landscape.

I love to write workbooks because I have witnessed first hand that personal learning is in the DOING. In my career as a professional coach, I focused on taking action and turning insights into meaningful outcomes with my clients for over twenty years. The bottom line? DOING is a more fun way to learn.

We all have a different story of finding our Enneagram type. *I wonder what yours will be.*
Just like learning how to drive, the first kiss, or overcoming a challenge, our story is exactly our own experience. We get to watch our story unfold and we learn to be present to our experiences.

There is no failure, there is no "wrong." It is all a valuable part of the journey.
I hope I have woven these ideas throughout the FUNeagram™ workbook.

I adore the idea of exploring without judgment. This means keeping an open mind and heart to encourage growth without getting caught up in notions of right or wrong, good or bad. The 4-step process to find your type provides just the right amount of structure while also allowing room for discovery and learning in a free-flowing manner.

So, don't be surprised if you land on your type right away, feeling crystal clear and raising your arms in a moment of finite glory. And don't be surprised if you land in the valley with questions, maybe even with more than you knew you had. Maybe you are not sure. Maybe you are quite sure. **Welcome to your own journey. Your own story. What if you're exactly where you're supposed to be?**

In my work coaching hundreds of clients, the best outcomes are not WHAT the story is about, but HOW the story leads to the truth. It's about being able to see ourselves in action. That's where we gain the gold nuggets that matter. Not by just getting to the finish line of a particular answer.

The Enneagram is the perfect tool for self-discovery. I love helping people find meaning in the experience of discovering their type—whether they are hit-or-miss or somewhere in between the first time. They imagine being exactly where they're supposed to be. This is the greatest fulfillment and best opportunity for self-love. Accepting the true value of your own journey is what matters most.

Join the club of being awkward humans stumbling along together on the path of growth!

FUNeagram is 100% here to support your journey whether you are a newbie learning for the first time, or a pro wanting to share the Enneagram. It's your own river-of-life trip, your boat, and your choices.

Here is your team of FUNeagram types, as travel companions on your path:

FUNeagram 1 is making sure you have a good structure and a plan to work with.
FUNeagram 2 is cheering you on with positivity and support.
FUNeagram 3 is inviting you into your light with step-by-step efficiency.
FUNeagram 4 is nudging you into your inner landscape to meet your authenticity.
FUNeagram 5 is offering the curiosity you need to explore and learn.
FUNeagram 6 "has your back" and is guiding you to find the leadership you need.
FUNeagram 7 is reminding you how FUN this adventure truly is, and to go get more!
FUNeagram 8 is commanding you go in strong, keep it simple, and just be yourself.
FUNeagram 9 is holding the space for you to explore in a comfortable way.

Thank you for letting me share my passion for the Enneagram with you in this new way.

Put on your life jacket, pack your cooler with all you need, and here comes another marvelous day riding the river currents. Be present to all of it!

Jenifer Novak

Hello!

**You're probably an Enneagram enthusiast
(or about to be more of one!)
who loves personal growth, staying
curious, and living your best life while
making the most of this incredible
experience of being human.**

Take this workbook in hand as you walk your personal growth path
and dive into the exciting adventure of learning more about yourself.

Boost your wins at life with a keep-it-simple, break-it-down approach
to the ***best tool for self-discovery ever. . .***

The Enneagram!

Jenifer Novak
Creator of FUNeagram™

THE CARD DECK

IMPORTANT NOTE: This workbook features cards from the FUNeagram™ card deck. You will still get 100% VALUE from this workbook without having the card deck, but it would be great to use the full card deck along with it! Card images are pictured in this Workbook for reference.

 **CARD DECKS ARE AVAILABLE AT WWW.FUNEAGRAM.COM**

- **Full-color printed cards**
- **Deck contains 56 cards**
- **ACTUAL SIZE: 3.5" x 5.5"**

BONUS:
All of the cards used in the 4-Step process to find your Enneagram type are pictured at full size in this workbook.

WHAT'S THE FUN PART?

Fun is defined by diving headfirst into life with playfulness, connection, and a flow that ties everything together into one big fun-tastic experience!

How FUNeagram™ brings the FUN:

- **Simplifying**
- **Playful**
- **Creative**
- **Visual**
- **Re-framing**
- **Conceptual**
- **Ease**

A New Approach

Do you over-complicate and take yourself too seriously?
You are not alone. It's normal to feel overwhelmed or anxious about seeing parts of yourself that you have not faced or dealt with before.

FUNeagram™ supports being open and feeling safe to approach every step of your growth with an anticipation of inspiration, simplicity, light-hearted exploration, and great fulfillment!

Benefits of FUN:

- Learn to laugh at yourself.
- Enjoy appreciating new things in your everyday life.
- Make an effort to seek out and try new things.
- Find ways to make your work and relationships fun.
- Switch up your routine.

While the quest for self-understanding is complex, a simplified and step-by-step "how to proceed" is a useful start.

TABLE OF CONTENTS

INTRODUCTION

PART ONE

The 4-step Process to Find Your Type

MAKING THE COMPLEX SIMPLE

- **Tips, Tools, Worksheets, Exercises**
- **Step-by-Step Instructions**
- **Break-it-Down Visuals**

F FIND YOUR TYPE

Follow the FUNeagram™ 4-step process.

U UNDERSTAND THE ENNEAGRAM

- Learn the DESCRIPTIONS.
- Learn the MOTIVATIONS.
- Discover the GIFTS of each type.

N NEXT STEPS FOR GROWTH

- Use the ARROWS for directions to grow.
- Explore the WINGS to increase self awareness.
- Explore the TALKING STYLES to improve communication.

AND ADDITIONAL DISCOVERY!

- New tools for clarity about the types.
- Enneagram affirmations and how to use them.
- See the "Big Picture" of the Enneagram.
- How to use the Enneagram GIFTS, a step-by-step guide.
- FUNeagram Success Stories - real life examples.

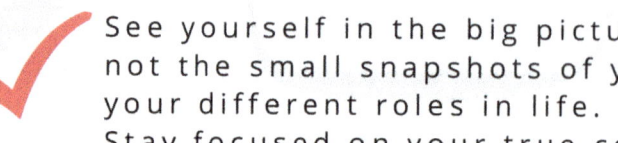
✓ See yourself in the big picture of your life, not the small snapshots of your past, or your different roles in life.
Stay focused on your true core self.

✓ Do not make choices based on how you "want" to be. Choose for the way you are naturally. No judgement.

✓ Give yourself grace and compassion at all times, and celebrate both the dark and light sides of your type as opportunities to grow and thrive.

✓ This is an ongoing exploration and practice. You cannot get it wrong. It's just another stepping stone on your path. So. . .*enjoy the forever journey!*

What is your goal or intention for this workbook?

HOW THE ENNEAGRAM WORKS

The Enneagram doesn't put you in a category, define you, and then leave you alone. . . *not at all.* It's your trusty map to escape the labels, the limiting categories, and find the true expression of all that you are. It's your trusty guide to discover how to use your insights and learnings to evolve into your best self.

Solving the mysteries of your inner self can feel like diving into the depths of your very soul, so let's kick things off with a simple step-by-step guide on where to begin.

The Enneagram is an ancient model that has evolved into being applied in diverse settings globally. It encompasses nine distinct types (or archetypes) based on motivations. Each type reflects a unique worldview that influences an individual's thoughts, emotions, and behaviors in their interactions with the world, others, and themselves.

The Enneagram (which is a Greek word meaning "diagram of nine") is divided into sections of 3, called "TRIADS." There are 3 types within each TRIAD.

EXPRESSION TRIAD - how we know or make sense of things.
COPING TRIAD - dealing with challenges or stress.
INTERACTION TRIAD- being with others, how we show up.

Through exploring the TRIADS we can see how all nine types are organized into the Enneagram framework.

While the Enneagram can be a life-long journey, this workbook is designed to be a great foundation to support you as deep and far as you want to go.

The FUNeagram™ simplifies and reveals the structure and organization of the basic elements of the Enneagram.

BODY EXPRESSION

HEART EXPRESSION

HEAD EXPRESSION

FIND YOUR TYPE IN 4 STEPS

1 Choose one EXPRESSION card.

2 Choose one CONFLICT card.

3 Choose one INTERACTION card.

4 Find your common color.

Choose one MOTIVATION card.

YOU FOUND YOUR TYPE

THE 4-STEP PROCESS SUMMARY

✓ First, you will **choose ONE single card** from each TRIAD. (Steps 1,2, and 3.)

✓ Next, you will see a common color among the cards you selected.

✓ Then, you will choose a MOTIVATION card to match the common color(s).

✓ The MOTIVATION CARDS bring clarity to what type fits you best. Narrow it down if you explore more than one common color.

The number on the MOTIVATION card is your type.

✓ **You have found your type!** (*or at least given yourself a strong start.*)

If you need to keep exploring to verify your type, you will use the DESCRIPTION cards for additional discovery.

© FUNEAGRAM 4

Example of the 4 Steps

1

EXPRESSION TRIAD

2

CONFLICT TRIAD

3

INTERACTION TRIAD

4

MOTIVATIONS

USE THE CARD IMAGES
ON THE FOLLOWING PAGES FOR STEPS 1 - 4

GETTING STARTED

PREPARE YOUR CARD IMAGES
TO USE AS YOU GO THROUGH THE STEPS.

Use Full Size Cards

Use a Reference Sheet

OPTION #1

Make a copy of the pages
with cards on them.
Cut out the cards to use
throughout the workbook.

OPTION #2

Tag the page for reference,
OR make a copy to use
throughout the workbook.

The signature 4-step process illuminates how to work with the Enneagram.

As you consider the steps, you'll find yourself immersed in more imaginative and creative thinking, making it easier to explore your inner world.

With solid organization the four steps guide you to find your type.

Whether you're a visual learner or enjoy a creative and interactive experience, the FUNeagram™ is sure to engage your mind and spark you into action.

Open up to a conversation with your higher self, and embark on an inspiring journey of self-discovery through the Enneagram.

Cards for Steps 1 - 4 are on the following 8 pages.

TRIAD CARDS

EXPRESSION TRIAD

HOW I KNOW BEST OR MAKE SENSE OF THINGS.

Body

MY STYLE IS:

TO BE PRODUCTIVE AND MAKE THINGS HAPPEN

I EMPHASIZE:

INSTINCT AND DOING

I RELY ON:

PHYSICAL SENSES AND BEING GROUNDED

OPTION TO COPY THE PAGES AND CUT OUT THE CARDS.

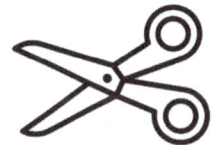

EXPRESSION TRIAD
HOW I KNOW BEST OR MAKE SENSE OF THINGS.

Head

MY STYLE IS:

DETAIL ORIENTED AND PLANNING

I EMPHASIZE:

MENTAL AND THINKING

I RELY ON:

PERCEPTIONS AND LOGIC

EXPRESSION TRIAD
HOW I KNOW BEST OR MAKE SENSE OF THINGS.

Heart

MY STYLE IS:

TO BE AWARE OF FEELINGS AND OTHERS

I EMPHASIZE:

EMOTIONS AND FEELINGS

I RELY ON:

AUTHENTICITY AND CONNECTION

INTERACTION TRIAD
HOW I GET WHAT I WANT FROM OTHERS

Against

MY STYLE IS:

TAKING ACTION, CREATING MOVEMENT, AND LEADING THE WAY

I EMPHASIZE:

BEING A STRONG PRESENCE

I RELY ON:

ACTIVELY TAKING CHARGE

INTERACTION TRIAD
HOW I GET WHAT I WANT FROM OTHERS

Away

MY STYLE IS:

TO PROCESS MY OWN THOUGHTS AND FEELINGS FIRST

I EMPHASIZE:

AN INWARD FOCUS OF MY ENERGY

I RELY ON:

MY INDEPENDENCE AND WITHDRAWING

INTERACTION TRIAD
HOW I GET WHAT I WANT FROM OTHERS

Toward

MY STYLE IS:

BEING SUPPORTIVE, IMPROVING, AND PROTECTING

I EMPHASIZE:

AN OUTWARD FOCUS OF MY ENERGY

I RELY ON:

ENGAGING AND COLLABORATING

CONFLICT TRIAD
HOW I DEAL WITH LOSS OR CHALLENGES

Reactive

MY STYLE IS:

FOCUSING ON FEELINGS AND ENERGY

I EMPHASIZE:

STRONG LIKES AND DISLIKES

I RELY ON:

LOOKING FOR AN EQUAL REACTION FROM OTHERS

CONFLICT TRIAD
HOW I DEAL WITH LOSS OR CHALLENGES

Positive

MY STYLE IS:

TO HELP OTHERS FEEL GOOD

I EMPHASIZE:

BEING UPLIFTING

I RELY ON:

BUILDING PEOPLE UP AND DENYING THERE IS A PROBLEM

CONFLICT TRIAD
HOW I DEAL WITH LOSS OR CHALLENGES

Objective

MY STYLE IS:

TO BE EFFECTIVE AND OBJECTIVE

I EMPHASIZE:

PUTTING MY FEELINGS ASIDE

I RELY ON:

THINKING THINGS THROUGH AND SOLVING PROBLEMS LOGICALLY

TRIAD CARDS - REFERENCE SHEET

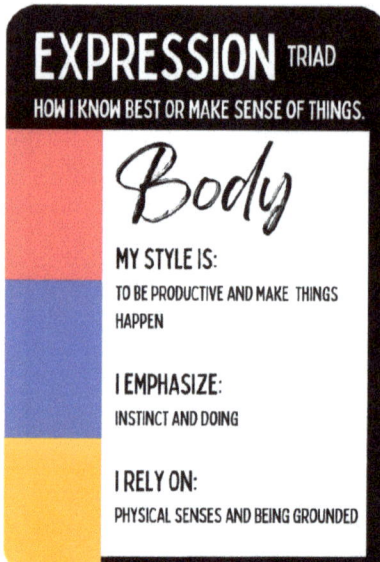

EXPRESSION TRIAD
HOW I KNOW BEST OR MAKE SENSE OF THINGS.

Body

MY STYLE IS:
TO BE PRODUCTIVE AND MAKE THINGS HAPPEN

I EMPHASIZE:
INSTINCT AND DOING

I RELY ON:
PHYSICAL SENSES AND BEING GROUNDED

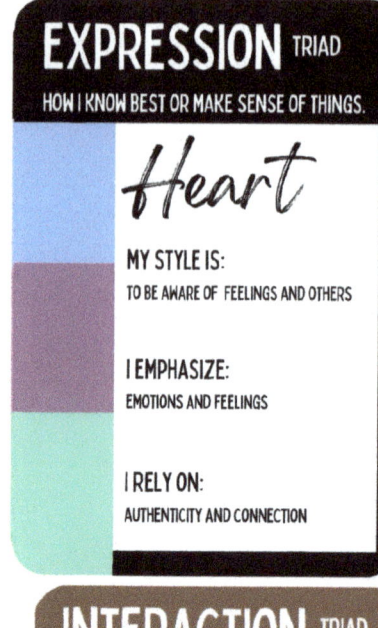

EXPRESSION TRIAD
HOW I KNOW BEST OR MAKE SENSE OF THINGS.

Heart

MY STYLE IS:
TO BE AWARE OF FEELINGS AND OTHERS

I EMPHASIZE:
EMOTIONS AND FEELINGS

I RELY ON:
AUTHENTICITY AND CONNECTION

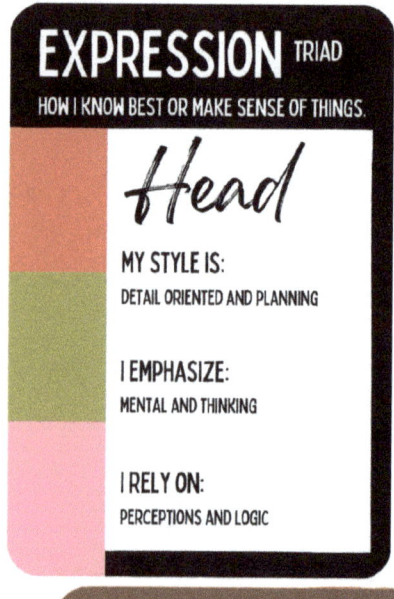

EXPRESSION TRIAD
HOW I KNOW BEST OR MAKE SENSE OF THINGS.

Head

MY STYLE IS:
DETAIL ORIENTED AND PLANNING

I EMPHASIZE:
MENTAL AND THINKING

I RELY ON:
PERCEPTIONS AND LOGIC

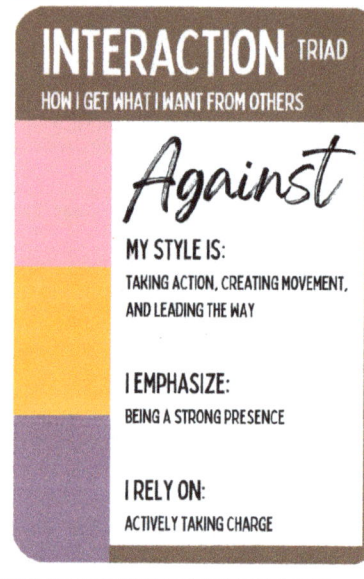

INTERACTION TRIAD
HOW I GET WHAT I WANT FROM OTHERS

Against

MY STYLE IS:
TAKING ACTION, CREATING MOVEMENT, AND LEADING THE WAY

I EMPHASIZE:
BEING A STRONG PRESENCE

I RELY ON:
ACTIVELY TAKING CHARGE

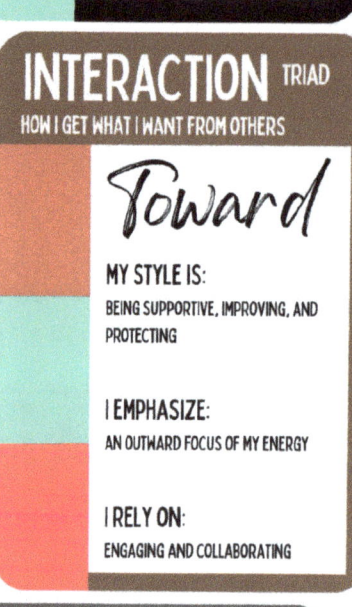

INTERACTION TRIAD
HOW I GET WHAT I WANT FROM OTHERS

Toward

MY STYLE IS:
BEING SUPPORTIVE, IMPROVING, AND PROTECTING

I EMPHASIZE:
AN OUTWARD FOCUS OF MY ENERGY

I RELY ON:
ENGAGING AND COLLABORATING

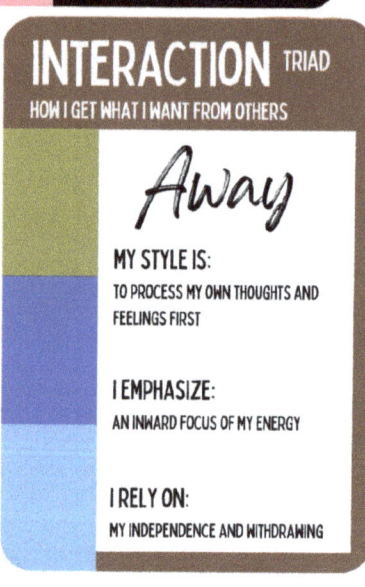

INTERACTION TRIAD
HOW I GET WHAT I WANT FROM OTHERS

Away

MY STYLE IS:
TO PROCESS MY OWN THOUGHTS AND FEELINGS FIRST

I EMPHASIZE:
AN INWARD FOCUS OF MY ENERGY

I RELY ON:
MY INDEPENDENCE AND WITHDRAWING

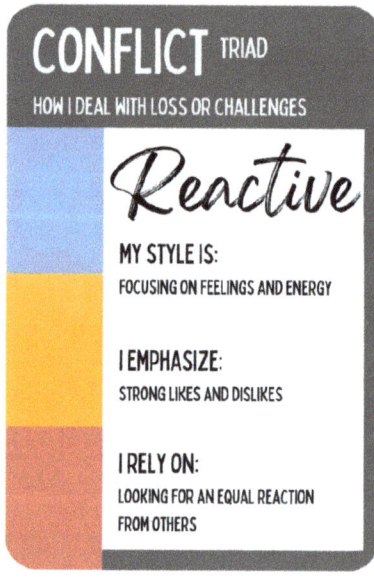

CONFLICT TRIAD
HOW I DEAL WITH LOSS OR CHALLENGES

Reactive

MY STYLE IS:
FOCUSING ON FEELINGS AND ENERGY

I EMPHASIZE:
STRONG LIKES AND DISLIKES

I RELY ON:
LOOKING FOR AN EQUAL REACTION FROM OTHERS

CONFLICT TRIAD
HOW I DEAL WITH LOSS OR CHALLENGES

Positive

MY STYLE IS:
TO HELP OTHERS FEEL GOOD

I EMPHASIZE:
BEING UPLIFTING

I RELY ON:
BUILDING PEOPLE UP AND DENYING THERE IS A PROBLEM

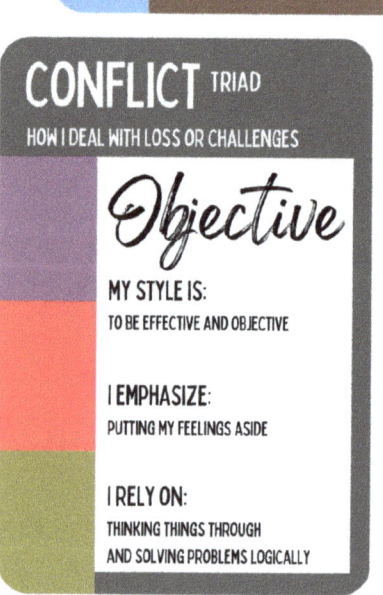

CONFLICT TRIAD
HOW I DEAL WITH LOSS OR CHALLENGES

Objective

MY STYLE IS:
TO BE EFFECTIVE AND OBJECTIVE

I EMPHASIZE:
PUTTING MY FEELINGS ASIDE

I RELY ON:
THINKING THINGS THROUGH AND SOLVING PROBLEMS LOGICALLY

MOTIVATION CARDS

MOTIVATION
- TO HAVE INTEGRITY
- TO BE A GOOD PERSON

....

- TO AVOID BEING WRONG
- TO AVOID BEING IRRESPONSIBLE

1 YOUR GIFT OR STRENGTH IS *Structure*

OPTION TO COPY THE PAGES AND CUT OUT THE CARDS.

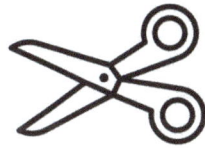

MOTIVATION

- TO FEEL LOVED
- TO BE LIKED + APPRECIATED

....

- TO AVOID FEELING UNWANTED
- TO AVOID BEING USELESS

2
YOU ARE THE GIFT OF
Service

MOTIVATION

- TO FEEL VALUABLE + WORTHWHILE
- TO OUTSHINE THE REST

....

- TO AVOID BEING INCAPABLE
- TO AVOID BEING EXPOSED

3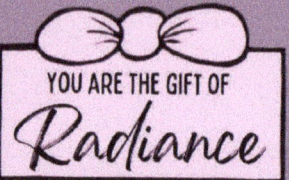
YOU ARE THE GIFT OF
Radiance

MOTIVATION

- TO BE UNIQUE + AUTHENTIC
- TO FIND DEEPER MEANING

....

- TO AVOID BEING ORDINARY
- TO AVOID EMOTIONAL DISCONNECTION

4
YOU ARE THE GIFT OF
Creativity

MOTIVATION

- TO BE KNOWLEDGABLE
- TO UNDERSTAND

....

- TO AVOID LOSS OF ENERGY
- TO AVOID INTRUSION BY OTHERS

5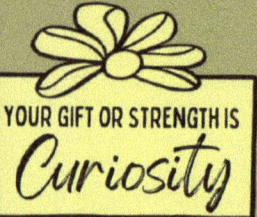
YOUR GIFT OR STRENGTH IS
Curiosity

MOTIVATION

- TO HAVE TRUST + CERTAINTY
- TO FIND GUIDANCE

....

- TO AVOID NEGATIVE SITUATIONS
- TO AVOID FEELING UNSAFE

6
YOUR GIFT OR STRENGTH IS
Prepared

MOTIVATION

- TO SEEK STIMULATION + PLEASURE
- TO FEEL SATISFIED

....

- TO AVOID PAIN + DISCOMFORT
- TO OPPOSE LIMITATIONS

7
YOU ARE THE GIFT OF
Adventure

MOTIVATION

- TO HAVE CONTROL + JUSTICE
- TO BE PROTECTIVE

....

- TO AVOID FEELING VULNERABLE
- TO AVOID BEING WEAK

8
YOU ARE THE GIFT OF
Strength

MOTIVATION

- TO HAVE HARMONY + COMFORT
- TO FIND INNER STABILITY

....

- TO AVOID DIRECT CONFLICT
- TO AVOID ILL WILL

9
YOU ARE THE GIFT OF
Harmony

MOTIVATION CARDS - REFERENCE SHEET

MOTIVATION
- TO HAVE INTEGRITY
- TO BE A GOOD PERSON

- TO AVOID BEING WRONG
- TO AVOID BEING IRRESPONSIBLE

1 YOUR GIFT OR STRENGTH IS *Structure*

MOTIVATION
- TO FEEL LOVED
- TO BE LIKED + APPRECIATED

- TO AVOID FEELING UNWANTED
- TO AVOID BEING USELESS

2 YOUR GIFT OR STRENGTH IS *Service*

MOTIVATION
- TO FEEL VALUABLE + WORTHWHILE
- TO BE EFFICIENT

- TO AVOID BEING INCAPABLE
- TO AVOID BEING EXPOSED

3 YOUR GIFT OR STRENGTH IS *Radiance*

MOTIVATION
- TO BE UNIQUE + AUTHENTIC
- TO FIND DEEPER MEANING

- TO AVOID BEING ORDINARY
- TO AVOID EMOTIONAL DISCONNECTION

4 YOUR GIFT OR STRENGTH IS *Creativity*

MOTIVATION
- TO BE KNOWLEDGABLE
- TO UNDERSTAND

- TO AVOID LOSS OF ENERGY
- TO AVOID INTRUSION BY OTHERS

5 YOUR GIFT OR STRENGTH IS *Curiosity*

MOTIVATION
- TO HAVE TRUST + CERTAINTY
- TO FIND GUIDANCE

- TO AVOID NEGATIVE SITUATIONS
- TO AVOID FEELING UNSAFE

6 YOUR GIFT OR STRENGTH IS *Prepared*

MOTIVATION
- TO SEEK STIMULATION + PLEASURE
- TO FEEL SATISFIED

- TO AVOID PAIN + DISCOMFORT
- TO OPPOSE LIMITATIONS

7 YOUR GIFT OR STRENGTH IS *Adventure*

MOTIVATION
- TO HAVE CONTROL + JUSTICE
- TO BE PROTECTIVE

- TO AVOID FEELING VULNERABLE
- TO AVOID BEING WEAK

8 YOU ARE THE GIFT OF *Strength*

MOTIVATION
- TO HAVE HARMONY + COMFORT
- TO FIND INNER STABILITY

- TO AVOID DIRECT CONFLICT
- TO AVOID OR PREVENT NEGATIVITY

9 YOUR GIFT OR STRENGTH IS *Harmony*

QUIZ *What's Your Style?*

Get ready for the 4-steps with this Quiz!
(Or, skip it and dive in to the next page!)

EXPRESSION TRIAD

When you want to take action, make a choice or make sense of something, what is your strongest tendency?

_____ Do I rely on my gut INSTINCT?
_____ Do I rely on what FEELS best?
_____ Do I rely on all I can KNOW?

CONFLICT TRIAD

If "the worst thing" happened, or a loss occured, how would you respond?

_____ My emotions and how I feel?
_____ My need to think and problem-solve?
_____ My desire to help others and myself to feel better about it?

INTERACTION TRIAD

When you are dealing with a social or group situation:

_____ Am I looking outward for collaboration/engagement?
_____ Am I looking inward for independence and self-reliance?
_____ Am I taking a strong position, or leading the situation?

Step 1 *Expression Triad*

CHOOSE ONE CARD THAT FITS YOU BEST

First
Imagine a specific situation like choosing a restaurant for a special occasion, or considering a job offer.

Instructions

CHOOSE ONE CARD TO DESCRIBE HOW YOU WOULD TAKE ACTION, MAKE A CHOICE, OR MAKE SENSE OF YOUR SITUATION.

☐ **"BODY"**
You relate most to being grounded, having a strong sense of what to do, and rely on your gut instincts.

☐ **"HEART"**
You relate most to what feels best, you rely on your emotions for a sense of clarity in your heart.

☐ **"HEAD"**
You relate most to logically processing things, having a clear perspective, and an objective way of thinking.

Step 2 *Conflict Triad*

CHOOSE ONE CARD THAT FITS YOU BEST

CONFLICT TRIAD
HOW I DEAL WITH LOSS OR CHALLENGES

Positive

MY STYLE IS:
TO HELP OTHERS FEEL GOOD

I EMPHASIZE:
BEING UPLIFTING

I RELY ON:
BUILDING PEOPLE UP AND
DENYING THERE IS A PROBLEM

CONFLICT TRIAD
HOW I DEAL WITH LOSS OR CHALLENGES

Objective

MY STYLE IS:
TO BE EFFECTIVE AND OBJECTIVE

I EMPHASIZE:
PUTTING MY FEELINGS ASIDE

I RELY ON:
THINKING THINGS THROUGH
AND SOLVING PROBLEMS LOGICALLY

CONFLICT TRIAD
HOW I DEAL WITH LOSS OR CHALLENGES

Reactive

MY STYLE IS:
FOCUSING ON FEELINGS AND ENERGY

I EMPHASIZE:
STRONG LIKES AND DISLIKES

I RELY ON:
LOOKING FOR AN EQUAL REACTION
FROM OTHERS

First

Imagine a specific situation like a family drama or an intense situation among friends or coworkers.

Instructions

CHOOSE ONE CARD TO DESCRIBE HOW YOU WOULD TAKE ACTION, MAKE A CHOICE, OR MAKE SENSE OF YOUR SITUATION.

☐ **"POSITIVE"**
You relate most to building
people up with
positivity or
taking a positive role to
improve the situation.

☐ **"OBJECTIVE"**
You relate most to thinking it through first, wanting to be effective with logic and objectivity.

☐ **"REACTIVE"**
You relate most to emotional reactions, looking for reactions from others, or becoming emotionally engaged in the situation.

Step 3 *Interaction Triad*

CHOOSE ONE CARD THAT FITS YOU BEST

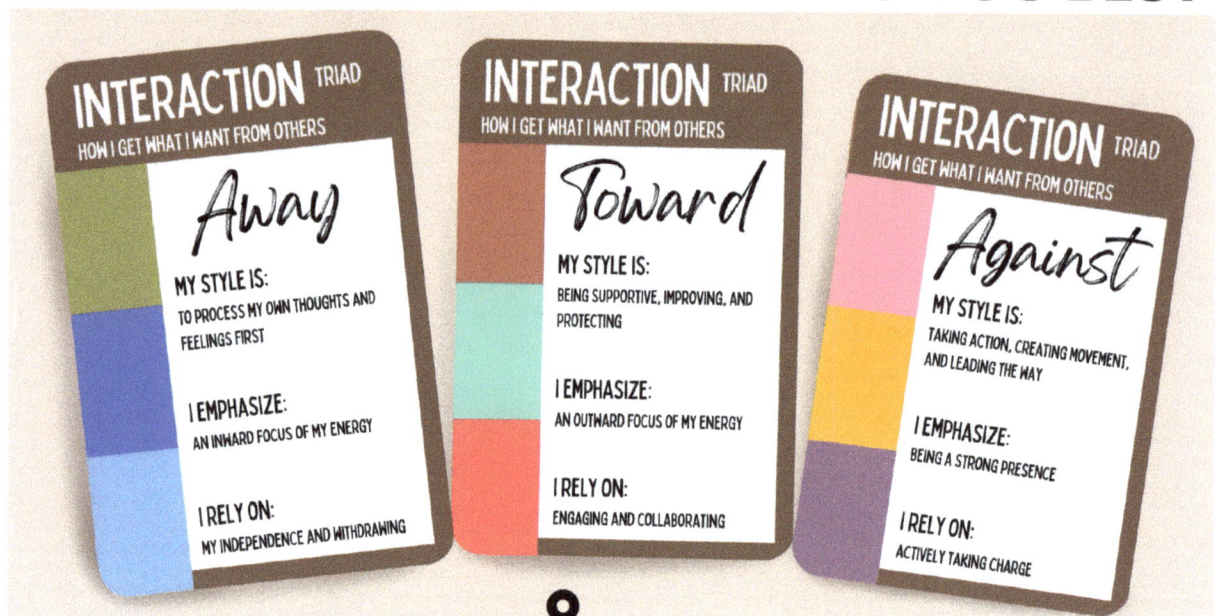

INTERACTION TRIAD
HOW I GET WHAT I WANT FROM OTHERS

Away

MY STYLE IS:
TO PROCESS MY OWN THOUGHTS AND FEELINGS FIRST

I EMPHASIZE:
AN INWARD FOCUS OF MY ENERGY

I RELY ON:
MY INDEPENDENCE AND WITHDRAWING

INTERACTION TRIAD
HOW I GET WHAT I WANT FROM OTHERS

Toward

MY STYLE IS:
BEING SUPPORTIVE, IMPROVING, AND PROTECTING

I EMPHASIZE:
AN OUTWARD FOCUS OF MY ENERGY

I RELY ON:
ENGAGING AND COLLABORATING

INTERACTION TRIAD
HOW I GET WHAT I WANT FROM OTHERS

Against

MY STYLE IS:
TAKING ACTION, CREATING MOVEMENT, AND LEADING THE WAY

I EMPHASIZE:
BEING A STRONG PRESENCE

I RELY ON:
ACTIVELY TAKING CHARGE

First
Imagine a specific situation like negotiating in a relationship, or how you get your needs met with others.

Instructions
CHOOSE ONE CARD TO DESCRIBE HOW YOU WOULD TAKE ACTION, MAKE A CHOICE, OR MAKE SENSE OF YOUR SITUATION.

☐ **"AWAY"**
You primarily withdraw or stay independent in situations with others. You want to process things on your own.

☐ **"TOWARD"**
You primarily involve or engage with others, looking for togetherness or collaboration.

☐ **"AGAINST"**
You primarily take leadership or want to be in charge of situations with others.

Review Your Choices

DID YOU CHOOSE 3 CARDS?

OR DO YOU HAVE TWO OPTIONS?

MY EXPRESSION CARD IS

MY INTERACTION CARD IS

MY CONFLICT CARD IS

MY OPTIONAL CARD IS

"What if I can't decide between two cards?"

It's okay to consider both!

Sometimes more than one style is expressed. But, for best results, you must choose ONE card only in at least one of the Triads.

Find Common Colors

(REFER TO THE COLOR BAR ON THE LEFT SIDE OF EACH CARD)

*Just focus on the colors, don't worry about types or numbers at this point.

Example #1

ONE COMMON COLOR = GOLD

TWO COMMON COLORS = GOLD+RED

Example #2

Here's another example where two cards are chosen instead of just one. You can see three common colors among all the chosen cards. **Keep going!**

HERE YOU SEE THREE COMMON COLORS TO CONSIDER IN STEP 4

© FUNEAGRAM 20

Step 4 *Motivations*

CHOOSE A MOTIVATION CARD IN YOUR COMMON COLOR

**MOTIVATIONS are a very important step to clarify your type.
The Enneagram is about WHY you do what you do. . .
not just a label of your behavior.**

**COMMON COLOR
= TEAL**

**COMMON COLOR
= PINK**

Example of more than one common color:

**In EXAMPLE #2 on the previous page,
you would choose these three
MOTIVATION cards to consider.**

Keep going to learn more!

Learn the MOTIVATIONS

WHEN YOU UNDERSTAND ALL NINE MOTIVATIONS
YOU WILL UNDERSTAND YOURSELF AND OTHERS MORE.

Imagine someone who always keeps their house clean and organized.
Go beyond the stereotype of labeling them as a "Neat Freak".
Ask yourself, *WHY are they doing it?*

There can be many different MOTIVATIONS for the same behavior.

COMPARE 3 MOTIVATIONS

MOTIVATION

- TO BE UNIQUE + AUTHENTIC
- TO FIND DEEPER MEANING

....

- TO AVOID BEING ORDINARY
- TO AVOID EMOTIONAL DISCONNECTION

4 — YOU ARE THE GIFT OF *Creativity*

MOTIVATION

- TO FEEL LOVED
- TO BE LIKED + APPRECIATED

....

- TO AVOID FEELING UNWANTED
- TO AVOID BEING USELESS

2 — YOU ARE THE GIFT OF *Service*

MOTIVATION

- TO SEEK STIMULATION + PLEASURE
- TO FEEL SATISFIED

....

- TO AVOID PAIN + DISCOMFORT
- TO OPPOSE LIMITATIONS

7 — YOU ARE THE GIFT OF *Adventure*

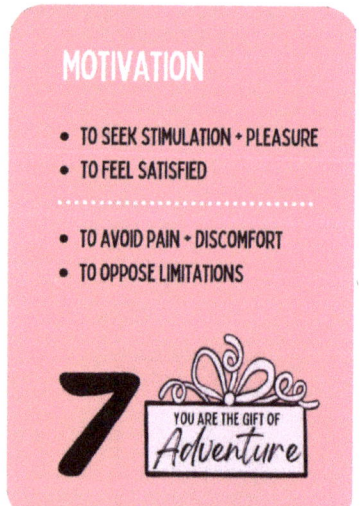

Type 4, *"When my house is clean I feel more creative. I have space for new or inspiring projects."*

Type 2, *"My friends will be more comfortable if my house is clean. People will appreciate me more.*

Type 7, *"I don't want to miss an opportunity for a party or doing something fun by having a messy house!"*

BECOMING MORE AWARE OF MOTIVATIONS
HELPS YOU BE AT CHOICE TO LIVE YOUR BEST LIFE.

Worksheet
LEARNING MOTIVATIONS

Imagine each type is choosing a different exercise routine.
Notice how different motivations influence the choices.

CHOICE #1: A personal trainer with accountability.
Type 1 - I want to be sure I'm doing it right. I want to do what I say I'm going to do.
Type 6 - I like having a buddy to workout with, I like having rules to follow.
Type 9 - I want the support. I like the comfort of a skilled trainer.
Type 4 - I appreciate a trainer who really gets me and my unique needs.

CHOICE #2: A group cardio or dance class.
Type 2 - I want to feel connected with others and I want to cheer them on.
Type 7 - I want it to feel like a fun party.
Type 3 - I like being in the front doing it the best.
Type 5 - If people respect my space and it makes sense, I'm in.

CHOICE #3: Treadmill with headphones on.
Type 5 - I want my own space, I like using the time to learn.
Type 4 - I want to play music that transports my soul.
Type 6 - It seems safe and I don't have to worry about something going wrong.
Type 8 - I like the independence and being in charge of how hard I go.

CHOICE #4: Yoga or pilates at a group studio
Type 9 - I want to feel grounded in myself, I like being in the flow.
Type 1 - I can monitor my own improvement knowing I am doing it correctly.
Type 2 - I can make it fun so the instructor and other students have fun too.
Type 8 - I like using my breath to feel powerful and in control of myself.

Two Questions to Ponder

1) What exercise routine would you choose and WHY?

2) What are some typical choices you make,
and can you see your motivations behind the choices?

Does the MOTIVATION card fit?
If Yes...Celebrate Your Type!

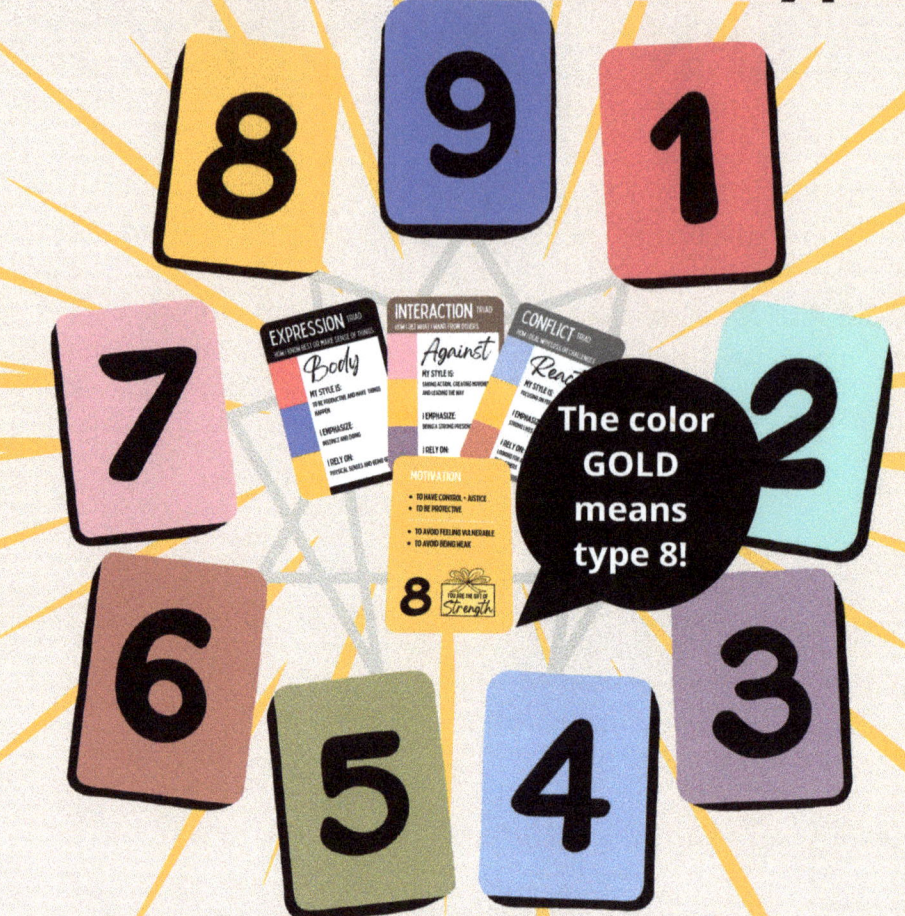

The color GOLD means type 8!

> *Ultimately, I am the only one who can identify myself with a certain type of the Enneagram. This process may move very quickly, or it may take a long time. I determine the tempo.*
>
> *Even those who don't immediately figure out their type can observe their own life story in the mirror of any type description and thereby make progress.*

Richard Rohr, "Grandfather of the Enneagram"

LEARN THE 9 TYPES

DESCRIPTION CARDS

Select DESCRIPTION cards in the colors you are considering.

Confirm your type when the DESCRIPTION card is a fit.

Study each DESCRIPTION card, noticing if you see the different qualities in yourself.
Learning all nine Enneagram types is your best move for growth.

DESCRIPTION CARDS - REFERENCE SHEET

DESCRIPTION
MY VIBE IS
Good
1
- DESIRES A MORE PERFECT WORLD.
- WORKS RELENTLESSLY TO IMPROVE OTHERS, THEMSELVES, AND EVERYTHING AROUND THEM.
- LOVES PLANS AND STRUCTURES FOR BEST RESULTS.

I WANT TO BE: MORAL + RESPONSIBLE
I RESIST BEING: BAD + MEDIOCRE

MY BEST SELF BELIEVES
"I Am Right-On"

DESCRIPTION
MY VIBE IS
Loving
2
- LOVES BEING LIKED BY OTHERS.
- ATTEMPTS TO FEEL WORTHY AND VALUED BY OFFERING GIFTS, ATTENTION, ADVICE AND RESOURCES TO OTHERS.
- HAS A WARM, NURTURING PRESENCE.

I WANT TO BE: THOUGHTFUL + GENEROUS
I RESIST BEING: SELFISH + INSENSITIVE

MY BEST SELF BELIEVES
"I Am Needed"

DESCRIPTION
MY VIBE IS
Effective
3
- LOVES TO BE RECOGNIZED FOR SUCCESS.
- SEEKS ADMIRATION THROUGH FOCUSING ON GOALS AND PLANS.
- HAS A SELF-ASSURED, CONFIDENT IMAGE.

I WANT TO BE: PROFESSIONAL + COMPETENT
I RESIST BEING: IDLE + INADEQUATE

MY BEST SELF BELIEVES
"I Am Successful"

DESCRIPTION
MY VIBE IS
Original
4
- PURSUES DEEP, AUTHENTIC AND UNBREAKABLE RELATIONSHIPS WITH THEMSELVES AND OTHERS.
- LOVES TO FIND AND CREATE MEANING, SYMBOLISM AND BEAUTY IN THE WORLD.

I WANT TO BE: CREATIVE + AUTHENTIC
I RESIST BEING: ORDINARY + BORING

MY BEST SELF BELIEVES
"I Am Special"

DESCRIPTION
MY VIBE IS
Wise
5
- LOVES TO ABSORB KNOWLEDGE IN AREAS THEY ARE PASSIONATE ABOUT.
- CAN BE HIGHLY CEREBRAL + LOGICAL.
- USUALLY EMOTIONALLY DETACHED AND VERY PRIVATE.

I WANT TO BE: COURAGEOUS + AUTONOMOUS
I RESIST BEING: EMOTIONAL + TRANSPARENT

MY BEST SELF BELIEVES
"I Am Knowledgable"

DESCRIPTION
MY VIBE IS
Loyal
6
- DESIRES TO ENABLE THE BEST OUTCOMES, AND TO PREVENT THE WORST OUTCOMES.
- CAN BECOME ANXIOUS ANTICIPATING WHAT MIGHT GO WRONG.
- LOVES OFFERING CARE AND RESPONSIBILITY.

I WANT TO BE: RELIABLE + CONSISTENT
I RESIST BEING: UNTRUSTWORTHY + DIFFICULT

MY BEST SELF BELIEVES
"I Am Safe"

DESCRIPTION
MY VIBE IS
Joyful
7
- LOVES TO EXPERIENCE EVERYTHING POSSIBLE THAT IS NEW AND EXCITING.
- REBELS AGAINST LIMITS OR RESTRAINTS.
- CAN EXPERIENCE LIFE AT A FASTER PACE THAN OTHERS.

I WANT TO BE: OPTIMISTIC + ENTHUSIASTIC
I RESIST BEING: TRAPPED + PESSIMISTIC

MY BEST SELF BELIEVES
"I Am Abundant"

DESCRIPTION
MY VIBE IS
Powerful
8
- DESIRES TRUTH, FAIRNESS AND SITUATIONS TO BE UNDER CONTROL.
- SHOWS UP AS BOLD AND EMPOWERED.
- PERCEIVES THINGS IN BLACK AND WHITE WITH MINIMAL GRAY AREA.

I WANT TO BE: INVINCIBLE + FORCEFUL
I RESIST BEING: WEAK + VULNERABLE

MY BEST SELF BELIEVES
"I Am Competent"

DESCRIPTION
MY VIBE IS
Peaceful
9
- AVOIDS CONFLICT AND SEEKS PEACE AND HARMONY.
- DOESN'T READILY ACCESS OR EXPRESS THEIR OWN POINT OF VIEW.
- EMBRACES MULTIPLE PERSPECTIVES.

I WANT TO BE: EASY GOING + ACCEPTING
I RESIST BEING: PUSHY + AMBITIOUS

MY BEST SELF BELIEVES
"I Am Comfortable"

Worksheet
DESCRIPTIONS

The more you understand all the types, the more you'll understand the power of using the Enneagram in your life/work/relationships.

What type inspires you most? And why?

What type do you resist or reject most? And why?

What have you learned about yourself by comparing the Descriptions of all the types?

FUNeagram™ Success Stories

Let's hear from all nine types about wins, challenges, insights, overcoming limitations, and ways to love ourselves more.

Cheers to success!

A mom finds out she's an Enneagram one and resists the stereotype that she's a controlling perfectionist!

Venturing deeper into her type, she realized her sage advice was just her way of sprinkling love and support everywhere. She uncovered a treasure chest of traits showing that her guiding light was fueled by a heart bursting with care.

Rather than seeing herself as a control freak, she embraced type one as a badge of honor reflecting her kindness and unwavering commitment to lifting up those in her orbit.

With newfound insight and a commitment to more self-love, she transformed her resistance into rays of positivity, nurturing growth and empowerment within herself.

Now she's loving her new ways to be on a mission to help others shine.

FUNeagram™ Success Stories

Jerry is a guy whose love life was like a roller coaster due to his over-the-top giving nature.

Enter type two, the hero that intercepted his romantic failures!

On Jerry's quest for self-awareness, he uncovered that his excessive giving was a plea for approval and love. Thanks to some Enneagram type two magic, he grasped the art of setting boundaries and finally allowed himself to receive love and care in return.

Armed with this epiphany, he kick-started a journey towards healthier relationships, infused with respect and genuine bonds.

By learning how to ask for his own needs, and finding equilibrium between giving and receiving, he set off on a new adventure of personal growth and contentment in both his relationships and his personal happiness.

Now he's being more true to himself and enjoying a stable loving relationship.

A tale of a smart business pro fixated on flaunting his achievements instead of tuning in to heartfelt conversations.

Max was always one to showcase himself, whether it was landing a big promotion at work or reaching a personal goal. While his drive and ambition were admirable, his focus on external success often overshadowed the importance of connecting on a deeper level with those around him.

Through the lens of Enneagram 3, Max had embodied "The Achiever." He was driven by a desire to succeed, be recognized, and constantly strive for improvement.

Once he started to understand the value of listening, empathizing, and being present in conversations, his relationships improved.

He learned that building meaningful connections brought a richness to his life that no amount of external success could match.

FUNeagram™ Success Stories

No wonder we click! We knew each other for our deep and introspective natures, and we both worked on seeing our emotions not as our masters but rather our companions in life.

Here's the twist – she rocks the type 3 wing while I soar with the type 5 wing. How can we be the same type but are SO different?

We were amazed how the Enneagram wings influenced our type in such unique ways! Embracing the different wings brought a beautiful balance to our friendship.

My friend's type 3 wing brought her a spark of motivation and drive, while my type 5 wing offers depth and introspection.

My best friend and I discovered we're both Enneagram type 4's!

Now we can celebrate our same yet different styles and learn from each other's perspectives – that's what makes our bond even more special!

When Joanna landed on type 5, she chuckled, "Ah, that explains why friends tease me about being the Question Queen!"

Now, she's on a mission to embrace her insatiable curiosity without driving her pals crazy. Embracing her newfound self-awareness, Joanna dove deeper into understanding her Enneagram type 5 traits.

She learned to appreciate her thirst for knowledge and analytical nature, realizing that her curiosity was a gift rather than a nuisance. Joanna found a balance between satisfying her intellectual appetite and engaging in meaningful conversations with her friends.

She discovered that being the "Question Queen" not only enriched her own life but also sparked intriguing discussions and brought fresh perspectives to those around her.

With a smile, she realized her Enneagram type was not just a label but a pathway to self-acceptance and personal growth.

FUNeagram™ Success Stories

Stella and her mom dove into the Enneagram world, discovering their types together.

Stella is a type 6 while Mom identified as type 4. Now they understand why they clash and don't always see eye to eye!

Mom would ask, *"Why do you have to be so worried?"* and Stella would ask, *"Why do you have to be so intense?"*

Their types opened up a new level of understanding and compassion between mother and daughter. They realized their differences in approaching life were rooted in their unique personalities.

Stella's cautious and loyal nature clashed with her mom's deep emotions and individualism. Yet, instead of causing more conflict, this realization brought them closer together.

They learned to communicate better. Stella can see her mom's intensity as passion and creativity, while mom understands Stella's worry as a form of care and responsibility.

They found a new appreciation for the complexities making them who they are.

Chris loves the type 7 vibe until dealing with the challenges of feeling caged by almost everything.

Chris said just by stopping enough to look in the mirror of type 7 they could step out of their default to always run from fear.

"And don't get me started on the struggle of mentally racing ahead of the pack, even though I know a slower dance is what would bring much more fulfillment" they said.

Chris' revelation sparked a new perspective that feeling limited wasn't always true, and it was costing them a lot of inner peace.

As Chris continued their journey of self-discovery, they learned to balance the desire for adventure with the importance of being centered in the present moment.

The challenges of type 7 no longer felt like a trap but rather a portal to understanding.

Now Chris can balance spontaneity with serenity, knowing both are essential.

FUNeagram™ Success Stories

When Joel discovered type 8, it was a light bulb moment! He is the boss-man on the outside, but inside he's just a big teddy bear!

Suddenly everything made sense - his inner powerhouse vibes and his secret superhero urge to save the day. How can Joel express his power without fearing the outcome?

Enneagram type 8 reveals that strength isn't about being bossy, but about being more like a guardian angel. Joel's protective nature and need for control are driven by loyalty and kindness.

By flipping his power switch to positivity, Joel can turn his strength into a superpower for making the world a brighter place.

Embracing his inner care-bear, Joel can bring love and empowerment wherever he goes, all while staying true to himself.

Now his attractive leadership style is bold and assertive because he knows he just wants to shield everyone with love.

Most people wouldn't know Maria often feels stuck in a whirlpool of indecision, drowning in the sea of "what's next?"

Maria is a type 9, and is stuck figuring out how to kickstart her engine and get moving! Embracing the 9 qualities allowed her to realize that being adrift in a sea of choices is totally normal.

This insight helps her take charge of what she really wants and that she can take a stand for what is important .

Maria accepted the challenge to simply take baby steps or set bite-sized goals. It's like setting sail on a tiny boat that will grow into a mighty ship of decision-making prowess!

The Enneagram gave her permission to feel positive about her ways, rather than feeling like something's wrong with her. Now she's got all the tools to sail through the fog of doubt with style and strength.

Finding inner stability inspired Maria to trust her gut and gear up for an exciting journey ahead!

TALKING STYLES

Word choices, comments and ways of communicating reveal the unique expression of the different types.

It's FUN to look for nuances in the way people talk.

TALKING STYLE cards can give you a new perspective or a helpful understanding of where people are coming from.

Keep it light, because there are MANY more talking styles, or combinations of talking styles that are not represented here.

Explore your matching colors from steps 1-4 to get more clarity on your type.

TIP: Improve your communication with others by learning the TALKING STYLES. Expand your choices for how to communicate and how to connect better with people using the different styles.

TALKING STYLE CARDS - REFERENCE SHEET

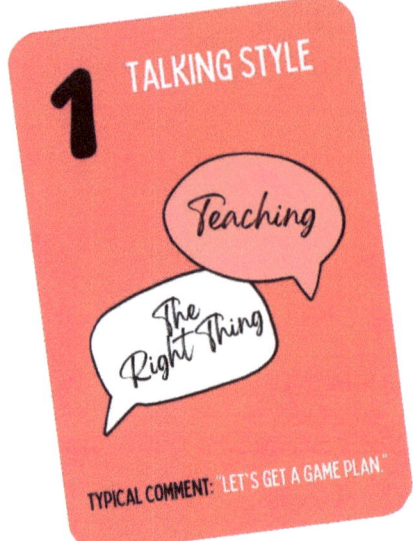

1 TALKING STYLE

Teaching

The Right Thing

TYPICAL COMMENT: "LET'S GET A GAME PLAN."

2 TALKING STYLE

Helping

Giving Advice

TYPICAL COMMENT: "I'D BE HAPPY TO."

3 TALKING STYLE

Self-Promoting

Publicity

TYPICAL COMMENT: "ABSOLUTELY I CAN DO IT."

4 TALKING STYLE

Romanticize

Longing

TYPICAL COMMENT: "I FEEL YOU."

5 TALKING STYLE

Analytical

Discourse

TYPICAL COMMENT: "LET ME EXPLAIN."

6 TALKING STYLE

Following Rules

Catastrophize

TYPICAL COMMENT: "I'VE GOT YOU COVERED."

7 TALKING STYLE

The Next Thing.

Storytelling

TYPICAL COMMENT: "IT'S ALL GOOD."

8 TALKING STYLE

Challenging

Big. Broad Statements

TYPICAL COMMENT: "I CAN HANDLE THIS."

9 TALKING STYLE

Long Narrative

Saga

TYPICAL COMMENT: "EVERYTHING WILL BE OK."

Worksheet
TALKING STYLES

Imagine you attended a wedding or a big event.
Explore different TALKING STYLES with the following prompts.

Describe the event based on the emotion and how you felt.

Describe the event being objective and what you thought about it.

Describe the event activities, giving a sense of what happened.

What styles are you most and least comfortable with and why?

ARROWS AND WINGS

- Expanding Your Inner Glow
- Transforming Vulnerability into Strength/Resilience
- Embracing the Joy and Beauty in Your Life

**EXAMPLE: TYPE 8
HAS ARROWS 5 AND 2**

The connecting lines in the center diagram are your two ARROWS.

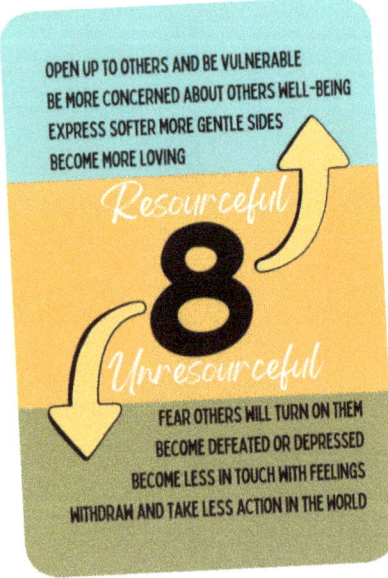

OPEN UP TO OTHERS AND BE VULNERABLE
BE MORE CONCERNED ABOUT OTHERS WELL-BEING
EXPRESS SOFTER MORE GENTLE SIDES
BECOME MORE LOVING

Resourceful

8

Unresourceful

FEAR OTHERS WILL TURN ON THEM
BECOME DEFEATED OR DEPRESSED
BECOME LESS IN TOUCH WITH FEELINGS
WITHDRAM AND TAKE LESS ACTION IN THE WORLD

**EXAMPLE: TYPE 2
HAS WINGS 1 AND 3**

The two numbers on either side of your type are your WINGS.

WINGS

2

QUALITIES TO SUPPORT
HEALTHY RELATIONSHIPS

- SUPPORTIVE
- STRUCTURED
- RESERVED

QUALITIES TO SUPPORT
LEADERSHIP AND HOSTING

- AMBITIOUS
- CHARMING
- ALTRUISTIC

Use Both Wings

1 WING : BEING DISCERNING
3 WING : STEPPING INTO EMPOWERMENT

ARROWS CARDS - REFERENCE SHEET

7

BECOME SELF-ACCEPTING AND OPTIMISTIC
PLAN ACTIVITIES FOR ENJOYMENT
FEEL SPONTANEOUS AND NATURAL
BECOME LESS CRITICAL

Resourceful

1

Unresourceful

LOSE SELF TRUST
LONG FOR WHAT'S MISSING
FEEL UNLOVEABLE AND UNLOVED
TURN ANGER INWARD (DEPRESSED)

4

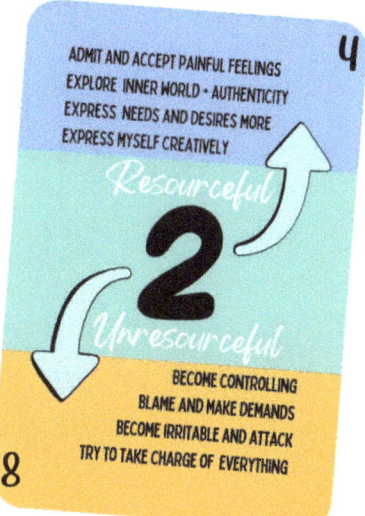

4

ADMIT AND ACCEPT PAINFUL FEELINGS
EXPLORE INNER WORLD + AUTHENTICITY
EXPRESS NEEDS AND DESIRES MORE
EXPRESS MYSELF CREATIVELY

Resourceful

2

Unresourceful

BECOME CONTROLLING
BLAME AND MAKE DEMANDS
BECOME IRRITABLE AND ATTACK
TRY TO TAKE CHARGE OF EVERYTHING

8

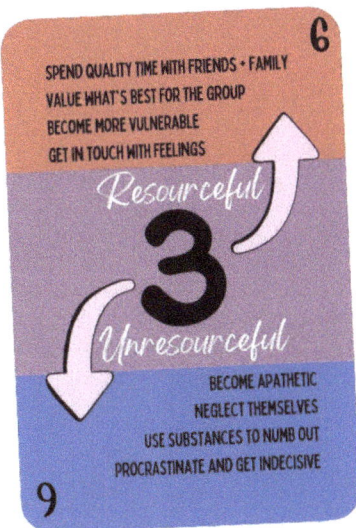

6

SPEND QUALITY TIME WITH FRIENDS + FAMILY
VALUE WHAT'S BEST FOR THE GROUP
BECOME MORE VULNERABLE
GET IN TOUCH WITH FEELINGS

Resourceful

3

Unresourceful

BECOME APATHETIC
NEGLECT THEMSELVES
USE SUBSTANCES TO NUMB OUT
PROCRASTINATE AND GET INDECISIVE

9

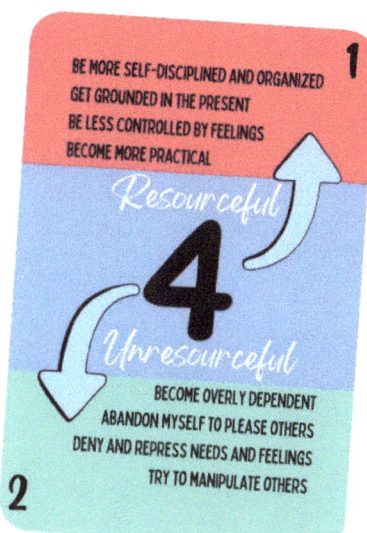

1

BE MORE SELF-DISCIPLINED AND ORGANIZED
GET GROUNDED IN THE PRESENT
BE LESS CONTROLLED BY FEELINGS
BECOME MORE PRACTICAL

Resourceful

4

Unresourceful

BECOME OVERLY DEPENDENT
ABANDON MYSELF TO PLEASE OTHERS
DENY AND REPRESS NEEDS AND FEELINGS
TRY TO MANIPULATE OTHERS

2

8

FEEL ENERGIZED BY ANGER VS. WITHDRAWING
BECOME MORE OUTSPOKEN AND SPONTANEOUS
SET CLEAR LIMITS + SELF-ADVOCATE
TRUST MY INSTINCTS

Resourceful

5

Unresourceful

BE EASILY DISTRACTED
TAKE ON TOO MANY NEW PROJECTS
BECOME MENTALLY SCATTERED
BECOME IMPULSIVE WITH THOUGHTS + ACTIONS

7

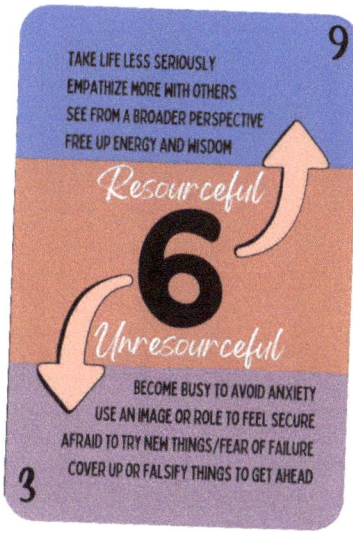

9

TAKE LIFE LESS SERIOUSLY
EMPATHIZE MORE WITH OTHERS
SEE FROM A BROADER PERSPECTIVE
FREE UP ENERGY AND WISDOM

Resourceful

6

Unresourceful

BECOME BUSY TO AVOID ANXIETY
USE AN IMAGE OR ROLE TO FEEL SECURE
AFRAID TO TRY NEW THINGS/FEAR OF FAILURE
COVER UP OR FALSIFY THINGS TO GET AHEAD

3

5

PLACE MORE VALUE ON WISDOM + SELF DISCIPLINE
BECOME QUIETER AND MORE INTROSPECTIVE
ACCEPT THE POLARITIES OF LIFE
GET IN TOUCH WITH FEARS

Resourceful

7

Unresourceful

BE JUDGEMENTAL OF SELF + OTHERS
BE OBSESSIVE ABOUT IDEAS + PROJECTS
BLAME OTHERS FOR PREVENTING FUN
BECOME CRITICAL, TRY TO CHANGE PEOPLE

1

1

OPEN UP TO OTHERS AND BE VULNERABLE
BE MORE CONCERNED ABOUT OTHERS WELL-BEING
EXPRESS SOFTER MORE GENTLE SIDES
BECOME MORE LOVING

Resourceful

8

Unresourceful

FEAR OTHERS WILL TURN ON THEM
BECOME DEFEATED OR DEPRESSED
BECOME LESS IN TOUCH WITH FEELINGS
WITHDRAW AND TAKE LESS ACTION IN THE WORLD

5

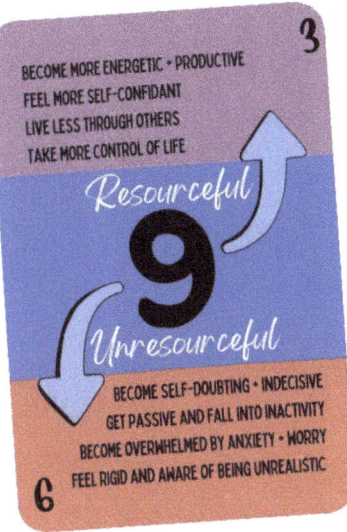

3

BECOME MORE ENERGETIC + PRODUCTIVE
FEEL MORE SELF-CONFIDANT
LIVE LESS THROUGH OTHERS
TAKE MORE CONTROL OF LIFE

Resourceful

9

Unresourceful

BECOME SELF-DOUBTING + INDECISIVE
GET PASSIVE AND FALL INTO INACTIVITY
BECOME OVERWHELMED BY ANXIETY + WORRY
FEEL RIGID AND AWARE OF BEING UNREALISTIC

6

ENNEAGRAM ARROWS

Arrows show what you can reach toward to bring out your best, and what you can work on when you are NOT at your best.

Your Resourceful Side

Resourceful is a state of well-being, functioning at your best, being on track, and having a full tank.

Your Unresourceful Side

Unresourceful is a state of stress, overwhelm, or running on empty, and functioning below your best.

Both are equally informative and valuable to explore. You will always experience both sides, it's a natural part of being human.

**If you aren't aware of the mud puddles
you could fall into, how will you successfully step over
them or be able to get out of them quicker and easier?**

GROW WITH ARROWS

Each Enneagram type is connected with two other types through the lines in the diagram known as ARROWS.

Learning the ARROWS gives you examples of the high and low side of the types you are connected to. Increase your self-awareness by exploring these possibilities within yourself.

Use the ARROWS to grow toward your high side and to let go of what doesn't serve you in your low side.

Each Enneagram type has it's own high side and low side. This practice of looking for what patterns you have in your behavior gives you space to make new choices.

GROW WITH ARROWS

COMBINE MOTIVATIONS WITH ARROWS

MORE F-U-N:
U - Understand yourself more by noticing what drives you to behave in certain ways. Now you can make new choices!

Select the MOTIVATION cards matching the colors of your ARROWS. Notice how being either **Resourceful** or **UNresourceful** is influenced by either a positive motivation or an avoidant motivation.

ARROWS cards help you have more compassion by understanding these different sides of yourself and others.

BONUS: For even deeper exploration, review the DESCRIPTION card for your UNresourceful patterns and find ways to transform your stress into strength.

Worksheet
UNDERSTANDING ARROWS

Pick one quality of your UNresourceful side.
How does this show up in your life?

Pick one quality of your Resourceful side.
How does this show up in your life?

How are your Arrows opportunities for growth?

What have you learned about yourself from your Arrows?

ENNEAGRAM WINGS

WINGS are one of many elements that give you a taste of complexity in the Enneagram.

Remember, the Enneagram is not a run-of-the-mill typing system, it's a complex blueprint that celebrates each person's quirks and charms in a unique way.

Let the WINGS be a fun entry into more self-discovery.

Each type has a number to the right and left side on the diagram called WINGS. The two WINGS influence how you uniquely express your core type.

You can use one WING dominantly, or you can equally use both. WINGS add depth and richness to your type as if they are different flavors brought into your core self.

Self-awareness is power. Study the qualities of both WINGS for insights and new possibilities.

WINGS CARDS - REFERENCE SHEET

WINGS 1

9 **2**

QUALITIES TO SUPPORT A POSITIVE OUTLOOK
- CALM
- BALANCED
- JUDICIAL

QUALITIES TO SUPPORT COMPASSION TOWARD OTHERS
- EMPATHETIC
- SUPPORTIVE
- WARM

Use Both Wings

9 WING: EMBRACE MULTIPLE PERSPECTIVES
2 WING: FOCUS ON ADVOCATING OUTWARDLY

WINGS 2

1 **3**

QUALITIES TO SUPPORT HEALTHY RELATIONSHIPS
- SUPPORTIVE
- STRUCTURED
- RESERVED

QUALITIES TO SUPPORT LEADERSHIP AND HOSTING
- AMBITIOUS
- CHARMING
- ALTRUISTIC

Use Both Wings

1 WING: BEING DISCERNING
3 WING: STEPPING INTO EMPOWERMENT

WINGS 3

2 **4**

QUALITIES TO SUPPORT CHARM AND RELATABILITY
- AMBITIOUS
- ENCHANTING
- CONFIDENT

QUALITIES TO SUPPORT EXPERTISE AND AUTHENTICITY
- FOCUS
- SERIOUS
- DEFINED

Use Both Wings

2 WING: HAVING EMPATHY AND MOTIVATING OTHERS
4 WING: EXPRESSING EMOTIONS AND SENSITIVITY

WINGS 4

3 **5**

QUALITIES TO SUPPORT RADIANT ASSERTIVENESS
- AUTHENTIC
- CONNECTED
- BELOVED

QUALITIES TO SUPPORT INNER WISDOM WITH UNIQUENESS
- CREATIVE
- INTROSPECTIVE
- INTELLECTUAL

Use Both Wings

3 WING: FOCUSING ON BEING EFFECTIVE
5 WING: SETTING CLEAR BOUNDARIES

WINGS 5

4 **6**

QUALITIES TO SUPPORT A PHILOSOPICAL PRESENCE
- CURIOUS
- RESERVED
- ATTENTIVE

QUALITIES TO SUPPORT PROBLEM-SOLVING
- LOGICAL
- PRACTICAL
- INDEPENDENT

Use Both Wings

4 WING: ACCESSING DEEPER FEELINGS
6 WING: PURSUING CONNECTION AND COMMITMENT

WINGS 6

5 **7**

QUALITIES TO SUPPORT GUARDIANSHIP
- INDEPENDENT
- HARD-WORKING
- LOGICAL

QUALITIES TO SUPPORT COMPANIONSHIP
- CARING
- RELIABLE
- SOCIABLE

Use Both Wings

5 WING: GAINING INNER AUTHORITY
7 WING: HAVING SPONTANEOUS FUN AND PLAYFULNESS

WINGS 7

6 **8**

QUALITIES TO SUPPORT BEING ENTERTAINING
- ENTHUSIASTIC
- LOYAL
- JOYFUL

QUALITIES TO SUPPORT SEIZING THE MOMENT
- CHARISMATIC
- PROTECTIVE
- OPTIMISTIC

Use Both Wings

6 WING: FACING YOUR FEARS AND BEING PRESENT
8 WING: BECOMING MORE GROUNDED AND DIRECT

WINGS 8

7 **9**

QUALITIES TO SUPPORT BEING INDEPENDENT
- IDEALISTIC
- ADVOCATING
- INSPIRING

QUALITIES TO SUPPORT BEING DIPLOMATIC
- CONFIDENT
- PATIENT
- PROTECTIVE

Use Both Wings

7 WING: PARTICIPATING WITH LIGHTNESS AND FREEDOM
9 WING: COMBINING STRENGTH WITH RECEPTIVITY

WINGS 9

8 **1**

QUALITIES TO SUPPORT ADVISING
- SOCIAL
- SUPPORTIVE
- OBJECTIVE

QUALITIES TO SUPPORT NEGOTIATING
- FRIENDLY
- OPTIMISTIC
- ORDERLY

Use Both Wings

8 WING: BEING ASSERTIVE AND TAKING CHARGE
1 WING: CREATING STRUCTURE AND MOTIVATION

GROW WITH WINGS

"QUALITIES TO SUPPORT..."
When each WING comes through your core type, it opens up certain strengths or possibilities. **For example, the qualities of the 1 WING support the possibility in type two to grow toward healthy relationships.**

MAIN QUALITIES (the three bullet points)
These are the outstanding qualities that support growth and add new flavors to your type.

"USE BOTH WINGS"
This section is a summary statement of how each WING can support you. Notice how the energy or the way it feels is quite different between the two WINGS.

Line up 10 people who are the same type, and you'll see 10 unique ways the WINGS are expressed. There are endless combinations of qualities making everyone's expression unique.

GROW WITH WINGS

COMBINE DESCRIPTIONS WITH WINGS

MORE F-U-N:

Add the DESCRIPTION cards to discover more about each WING.

Refer to the "I want to be" and "I resist being" section on the DESCRIPTION card to notice if you see any patterns around how you express the different qualities in your life.

Imagine taking on the "Vibe" of either type beside your number. The "My Vibe Is" section on the card describes the energy of how you show up.

Can you associate the vibe with the qualities of your wings? You can lean into both wings by choice.

BONUS: For more FUN. . .try reviewing the Gifts on the MOTIVATION cards to see how they expand your understanding of the WINGS.

TO SIMPLIFY: Maybe you just imagine each WING being an expression of that particular gift or strength.

Worksheet
UNDERSTANDING WINGS

What are 1-2 qualities in each Wing you are most attracted to?

How does each Wing give you a different approach to things?

What new perspective or insight do you get from either Wing?

Do you notice using one Wing more than the other? Why?

INTRODUCING COLLECTIVES

CARDS OF THE SAME COLOR FORM A COLLECTIVE FOR EACH TYPE.

Benefits of Collectives:

- **Understand others better**
- **Improve relationships**
- **Expand self-awareness**
- **Find compassion for self and others**

See the "BIG PICTURE" of each type.

COMPARE THE TYPES

A COLLECTIVE IS A GROUP OF 8 CARDS WITH ONE COMMON COLOR.

COLLECTIVE TYPE ONE

COLLECTIVE TYPE FOUR

TIPS FOR WORKING WITH COLLECTIVES

- Compare each card to explore similarities and differences between types.
- Study all nine collectives and try choosing your type by seeing which fits best.
- Explore the different styles on the TRIAD cards to learn how they are expressed differently through the types.

COLLECTIVES are on pages 49-57
WORKSHEETS are on pages 59-66

Type 1 Collective
The Reformer or Strict Perfectionist

DESCRIPTION
MY VIBE IS
Good

1

"DESIRES A MORE PERFECT WORLD AND WORKS RELENTLESSLY TO IMPROVE OTHERS, THEMSELVES AND EVERYTHING AROUND THEM."

I WANT TO BE: MORAL + RESPONSIBLE
I RESIST BEING: BAD + MEDIOCRE

AT MY BEST
"I am Right"

BECOME SELF-ACCEPTING AND OPTIMISTIC
PLAN ACTIVITIES FOR ENJOYMENT
FEEL SPONTANEOUS AND NATURAL
BECOME LESS CRITICAL

Resourceful

1

Unresourceful
LOSE SELF TRUST
LONG FOR WHAT'S MISSING
FEEL UNLOVEABLE AND UNLOVED
TURN ANGER INWARD (DEPRESSED)

MOTIVATION
- TO HAVE INTEGRITY
- TO BE A GOOD PERSON
- - - - - - - - - - -
- TO AVOID BEING WRONG
- TO AVOID BEING IRRESPONSIBLE

1
YOUR GIFT OR STRENGTH IS
Structure

---

1 **TALKING STYLE**

Teaching

The Right Thing

TYPICAL COMMENT: "LET'S GET A GAME PLAN."

WINGS

9 1 2

QUALITIES TO SUPPORT A POSITIVE OUTLOOK
- CALM
- BALANCED
- JUDICIAL

QUALITIES TO SUPPORT COMPASSION TOWARD OTHERS
- EMPATHETIC
- SUPPORTIVE
- WARM

Use Both Wings

9 WING: EMBRACE MULTIPLE PERSPECTIVES
2 WING: FOCUS ON ADVOCATING OUTWARDLY

EXPRESSION TRIAD
HOW I KNOW BEST OR MAKE SENSE OF THINGS

Body

MY STYLE IS:
TO BE PRODUCTIVE AND MAKE THINGS HAPPEN

I EMPHASIZE:
INSTINCT AND DOING

I RELY ON:
PHYSICAL SENSES AND BEING GROUNDED

CONFLICT TRIAD
HOW I DEAL WITH LOSS OR CHALLENGES

Objective

MY STYLE IS:
TO BE EFFECTIVE AND OBJECTIVE

I EMPHASIZE:
PUTTING MY FEELINGS ASIDE

I RELY ON:
THINKING THINGS THROUGH AND SOLVING PROBLEMS LOGICALLY

INTERACTION TRIAD
HOW I GET WHAT I WANT FROM OTHERS

Toward

MY STYLE IS:
BEING SUPPORTIVE, IMPROVING, AND PROTECTING

I EMPHASIZE:
AN OUTWARD FOCUS OF MY ENERGY

I RELY ON:
ENGAGING AND COLLABORATING

8 9 1
7 2
6 5 4 3

Type 2 Collective
The Helper or Considerate Giver

DESCRIPTION
MY VIBE IS
Loving
2
"DESIRES TO BE LIKED BY OTHERS AND ATTEMPTS TO FEEL WORTHY AND VALUED BY OFFERING GIFTS, ATTENTION, ADVICE AND RESOURCES TO OTHERS."

I WANT TO BE: THOUGHTFUL + GENEROUS
I RESIST BEING: SELFISH + INSENSITIVE

AT MY BEST
"I am Needed"

MOTIVATION
- TO FEEL LOVED
- TO BE LIKED + APPRECIATED

- TO AVOID FEELING UNWANTED
- TO AVOID BEING USELESS

2 YOUR GIFT OR STRENGTH IS
Service

ADMIT AND ACCEPT PAINFUL FEELINGS
EXPLORE INNER WORLD + AUTHENTICITY
EXPRESS NEEDS AND DESIRES MORE
EXPRESS MYSELF CREATIVELY
Resourceful
2
Unresourceful
BECOME CONTROLLING
BLAME AND MAKE DEMANDS
BECOME IRRITABLE AND ATTACK
TRY TO TAKE CHARGE OF EVERYTHING

TALKING STYLE
2
Helping
Giving Advice
TYPICAL COMMENT: "I'D BE HAPPY TO."

WINGS
1 2 3
QUALITIES TO SUPPORT HEALTHY RELATIONSHIPS
- SUPPORTIVE
- STRUCTURED
- RESERVED

QUALITIES TO SUPPORT LEADERSHIP AND HOSTING
- AMBITIOUS
- CHARMING
- ALTRUISTIC

Use Both Wings
1 WING: BEING DISCERNING
3 WING: STEPPING INTO EMPOWERMENT

EXPRESSION TRIAD
HOW I KNOW BEST OR MAKE SENSE OF THINGS.
Heart
MY STYLE IS:
TO BE AWARE OF FEELINGS AND OTHERS

I EMPHASIZE:
EMOTIONS AND FEELINGS

I RELY ON:
AUTHENTICITY AND CONNECTION

CONFLICT TRIAD
HOW I DEAL WITH LOSS OR CHALLENGES
Positive
MY STYLE IS:
TO HELP OTHERS FEEL GOOD

I EMPHASIZE:
BEING UPLIFTING

I RELY ON:
BUILDING PEOPLE UP AND DENYING THERE IS A PROBLEM

INTERACTION TRIAD
HOW I GET WHAT I WANT FROM OTHERS
Toward
MY STYLE IS:
BEING SUPPORTIVE, IMPROVING, AND PROTECTING

I EMPHASIZE:
AN OUTWARD FOCUS OF MY ENERGY

I RELY ON:
ENGAGING AND COLLABORATING

Type 3 Collective
The Performer or Competitive Achiever

MOTIVATION
- TO FEEL VALUABLE + WORTHWHILE
- TO BE EFFICIENT

- - - - - - - - - -

- TO AVOID BEING INCAPABLE
- TO AVOID BEING EXPOSED

3 YOUR GIFT OR STRENGTH IS *Radiance*

DESCRIPTION
MY VIBE IS
Effective
3 "DESIRES RECOGNITION FOR BEING SUCCESSFUL AND WORTHY OF ADMIRATION THROUGH FOCUSING ON GOALS AND PLANS, ALL WITH A SELF-ASSURED, CONFIDENT IMAGE".

I WANT TO BE: PROFESSIONAL + COMPETENT
I RESIST BEING: IDOL + INADEQUATE

AT MY BEST
"I am Successful"

SPEND QUALITY TIME WITH FRIENDS + FAMILY
VALUE WHAT'S BEST FOR THE GROUP
BECOME MORE VULNERABLE
GET IN TOUCH WITH FEELINGS
Resourceful
3
Unresourceful
BECOME APATHETIC
NEGLECT THEMSELVES
USE SUBSTANCES TO NUMB OUT
PROCRASTINATE AND GET INDECISIVE

3 **TALKING STYLE**
Self-Promoting
Publicity
TYPICAL COMMENT: "ABSOLUTELY I CAN DO IT."

WINGS
3
2   4
QUALITIES TO SUPPORT CHARM AND RELATABILITY
- AMBITIOUS
- ENCHANTING
- CONFIDENT

QUALITIES TO SUPPORT EXPERTISE AND AUTHENTICITY
- FOCUS
- SERIOUS
- DEFINED

Use Both Wings
2 WING: HAVING EMPATHY AND MOTIVATING OTHERS
4 WING: EXPRESSING EMOTIONS AND SENSITIVITY

EXPRESSION TRIAD
HOW I KNOW BEST OR MAKE SENSE OF THINGS
Heart
MY STYLE IS:
TO BE AWARE OF FEELINGS AND OTHERS

I EMPHASIZE:
EMOTIONS AND FEELINGS

I RELY ON:
AUTHENTICITY AND CONNECTION

CONFLICT TRIAD
HOW I DEAL WITH LOSS OR CHALLENGES
Objective
MY STYLE IS:
TO BE EFFECTIVE AND OBJECTIVE

I EMPHASIZE:
PUTTING MY FEELINGS ASIDE

I RELY ON:
THINKING THINGS THROUGH AND SOLVING PROBLEMS LOGICALLY

INTERACTION TRIAD
HOW I GET WHAT I WANT FROM OTHERS
Against
MY STYLE IS:
TAKING ACTION, CREATING MOVEMENT, AND LEADING THE WAY

I EMPHASIZE:
BEING A STRONG PRESENCE

I RELY ON:
ACTIVELY TAKING CHARGE

Type 4 Collective
The Individualist or Intense Creative

MOTIVATION
- TO BE UNIQUE + AUTHENTIC
- TO FIND DEEPER MEANING
- TO AVOID BEING ORDINARY
- TO AVOID EMOTIONAL DISCONNECTION

4 — YOUR GIFT OR STRENGTH IS *Creativity*

DESCRIPTION
MY VIBE IS *Original*
4 — "DESIRES A DEEP AUTHENTIC AND UNBREAKABLE RELATIONSHIP WITH THEMSELVES AND OTHERS, PURSUING MEANING, SYMBOLISM AND BEAUTY."

I WANT TO BE: CREATIVE + AUTHENTIC
I RESIST BEING: ORDINARY + BORING

AT MY BEST
"*I am Special*"

BE MORE SELF-DISCIPLINED AND ORGANIZED
GET GROUNDED IN THE PRESENT
BE LESS CONTROLLED BY FEELINGS
BECOME MORE PRACTICAL
Resourceful
4
Unresourceful
BECOME OVERLY DEPENDENT
ABANDON MYSELF TO PLEASE OTHERS
DENY AND REPRESS NEEDS AND FEELINGS
TRY TO MANIPULATE OTHERS

4 TALKING STYLE
Romanticize
Longing
TYPICAL COMMENT: "I FEEL YOU."

WINGS
3 — 4 — 5

QUALITIES TO SUPPORT RADIANT ASSERTIVENESS
- AUTHENTIC
- CONNECTED
- BELOVED

QUALITIES TO SUPPORT INNER WISDOM WITH UNIQUENESS
- CREATIVE
- INTROSPECTIVE
- INTELLECTUAL

Use Both Wings
3 WING: FOCUSING ON BEING EFFECTIVE
5 WING: SETTING CLEAR BOUNDARIES

EXPRESSION TRIAD
HOW I KNOW BEST OR MAKE SENSE OF THINGS.
Heart
MY STYLE IS:
TO BE AWARE OF FEELINGS AND OTHERS
I EMPHASIZE:
EMOTIONS AND FEELINGS
I RELY ON:
AUTHENTICITY AND CONNECTION

CONFLICT TRIAD
HOW I DEAL WITH LOSS OR CHALLENGES
Reactive
MY STYLE IS:
FOCUSING ON FEELINGS AND ENERGY
I EMPHASIZE:
STRONG LIKES AND DISLIKES
I RELY ON:
LOOKING FOR AN EQUAL REACTION FROM OTHERS

INTERACTION TRIAD
HOW I GET WHAT I WANT FROM OTHERS
Away
MY STYLE IS:
TO PROCESS MY OWN THOUGHTS AND FEELINGS FIRST
I EMPHASIZE:
AN INWARD FOCUS OF MY ENERGY
I RELY ON:
MY INDEPENDENCE AND WITHDRAWING

Type 5 Collective
The Investigator or Quiet Specialist

MOTIVATION
- TO BE KNOWLEDGABLE
- TO UNDERSTAND
- - - - - - - - - -
- TO AVOID LOSS OF ENERGY
- TO AVOID INTRUSION BY OTHERS

5 YOUR GIFT OR STRENGTH IS *Curiosity*

DESCRIPTION
MY VIBE IS *Wise*

5 "DESIRES TO ABSORB KNOWLEDGE IN AREAS THEY PERCEIVE IMPORTANT AND INTRIGUING, BECOMING HIGHLY CEREBERAL, EMOTIONALLY DETACHED AND VERY PRIVATE."

I WANT TO BE: COURAGEOUS + AUTONOMOUS
I RESIST BEING: EMOTIONAL + TRANSPARENT

AT MY BEST
"I am Knowledgable"

FEEL ENERGIZED BY ANGER VS. WITHDRAWING
BECOME MORE OUTSPOKEN AND SPONTANEOUS
SET CLEAR LIMITS + SELF-ADVOCATE
TRUST MY INSTINCTS
Resourceful
5
Unresourceful
BE EASILY DISTRACTED
TAKE ON TOO MANY NEW PROJECTS
BECOME MENTALLY SCATTERED
BECOME IMPULSIVE WITH THOUGHTS + ACTIONS

5 TALKING STYLE
Analytical
Discourse
TYPICAL COMMENT: "LET ME EXPLAIN."

WINGS
4 5 6
QUALITIES TO SUPPORT A PHILOSOPICAL PRESENCE
- CURIOUS
- RESERVED
- ATTENTIVE
QUALITIES TO SUPPORT PROBLEM-SOLVING
- LOGICAL
- PRACTICAL
- INDEPENDENT
Use Both Wings
4 WING: ACCESSING DEEPER FEELINGS
6 WING: PURSUING CONNECTION AND COMMITMENT

EXPRESSION TRIAD
HOW I KNOW BEST OR MAKE SENSE OF THINGS
Head
MY STYLE IS:
DETAIL ORIENTED AND PLANNING
I EMPHASIZE:
MENTAL AND THINKING
I RELY ON:
PERCEPTIONS AND LOGIC

CONFLICT TRIAD
HOW I DEAL WITH LOSS OR CHALLENGES
Objective
MY STYLE IS:
TO BE EFFECTIVE AND OBJECTIVE
I EMPHASIZE:
PUTTING MY FEELINGS ASIDE
I RELY ON:
THINKING THINGS THROUGH AND SOLVING PROBLEMS LOGICALLY

INTERACTION TRIAD
HOW I GET WHAT I WANT FROM OTHERS
Away
MY STYLE IS:
TO PROCESS MY OWN THOUGHTS AND FEELINGS FIRST
I EMPHASIZE:
AN INWARD FOCUS OF MY ENERGY
I RELY ON:
MY INDEPENDENCE AND WITHDRAWING

MOTIVATION

- TO HAVE TRUST + CERTAINTY
- TO FIND GUIDANCE

- TO AVOID NEGATIVE SITUATIONS
- TO AVOID FEELING UNSAFE

6 YOUR GIFT OR STRENGTH IS *Prepared*

DESCRIPTION
MY VIBE IS *Loyal*

6 "DESIRES TO ENABLE THE BEST TO MANIFEST AND THE WORST FROM OCCURING, WHILE ANTICIPATING SCENARIOS THAT MIGHT GO WRONG."

I WANT TO BE: RELIABLE + CONSISTENT
I RESIST BEING: UNTRUSTWORTHY + DIFFICULT

AT MY BEST
"I am Safe"

TAKE LIFE LESS SERIOUSLY
EMPATHIZE MORE WITH OTHERS
SEE FROM A BROADER PERSPECTIVE
FREE UP ENERGY AND WISDOM

Resourceful

6

Unresourceful
BECOME BUSY TO AVOID ANXIETY
USE AN IMAGE OR ROLE TO FEEL SECURE
AFRAID TO TRY NEW THINGS/FEAR OF FAILURE
COVER UP OR FALSIFY THINGS TO GET AHEAD

6 TALKING STYLE

Following Rules

Catastrophize

TYPICAL COMMENT: "I'VE GOT YOU COVERED."

WINGS

5 6 7

QUALITIES TO SUPPORT GUARDIANSHIP
- INDEPENDENT
- HARD-WORKING
- LOGICAL

QUALITIES TO SUPPORT COMPANIONSHIP
- CARING
- RELIABLE
- SOCIABLE

Use Both Wings
5 WING : GAINING INNER AUTHORITY
7 WING : HAVING SPONTANEOUS FUN AND PLAYFULNESS

EXPRESSION TRIAD
HOW I KNOW BEST OR MAKE SENSE OF THINGS.

Head

MY STYLE IS:
DETAIL ORIENTED AND PLANNING

I EMPHASIZE:
MENTAL AND THINKING

I RELY ON:
PERCEPTIONS AND LOGIC

CONFLICT TRIAD
HOW I DEAL WITH LOSS OR CHALLENGES

Reactive

MY STYLE IS:
FOCUSING ON FEELINGS AND ENERGY

I EMPHASIZE:
STRONG LIKES AND DISLIKES

I RELY ON:
LOOKING FOR AN EQUAL REACTION FROM OTHERS

INTERACTION TRIAD
HOW I GET WHAT I WANT FROM OTHERS

Toward

MY STYLE IS:
BEING SUPPORTIVE, IMPROVING, AND PROTECTING

I EMPHASIZE:
AN OUTWARD FOCUS OF MY ENERGY

I RELY ON:
ENGAGING AND COLLABORATING

Type 7 Collective
The Adventurer or Enthusiastic Visionary

DESCRIPTION

MY VIBE IS

Joyful

7

"DESIRES TO EXPERIENCE EVERYTHING POSSIBLE THAT IS NEW AND EXCITING WHILE REBELLING AGAINST LIMITS OR RESTRAINTS."

I WANT TO BE: OPTIMISTIC + ENTHUSIASTIC
I RESIST BEING: TRAPPED + PESSIMISTIC

AT MY BEST
"I am Abundant"

PLACE MORE VALUE ON WISDOM + SELF DISCIPLINE
BECOME QUIETER AND MORE INTROSPECTIVE
ACCEPT THE POLARITIES OF LIFE
GET IN TOUCH WITH FEARS

Resourceful

7

Unresourceful

BE JUDGEMENTAL OF SELF + OTHERS
BE OBSESSIVE ABOUT IDEAS + PROJECTS
BLAME OTHERS FOR PREVENTING FUN
BECOME CRITICAL, TRY TO CHANGE PEOPLE

MOTIVATION

- TO SEEK STIMULATION + PLEASURE
- TO FEEL SATISFIED

- TO AVOID PAIN + DISCOMFORT
- TO OPPOSE LIMITATIONS

7 YOUR GIFT OR STRENGTH IS
Adventure

---

7 TALKING STYLE

The Next Thing.

Storytelling

TYPICAL COMMENT: "IT'S ALL GOOD."

WINGS

7 6 8

QUALITIES TO SUPPORT BEING ENTERTAINING
- ENTHUSIASTIC
- LOYAL
- JOYFUL

QUALITIES TO SUPPORT SEIZING THE MOMENT
- CHARISMATIC
- PROTECTIVE
- OPTIMISTIC

Use Both Wings

6 WING: FACING YOUR FEARS AND BEING PRESENT
8 WING: BECOMING MORE GROUNDED AND DIRECT

EXPRESSION TRIAD
HOW I KNOW BEST OR MAKE SENSE OF THINGS.

Head

MY STYLE IS:
DETAIL ORIENTED AND PLANNING

I EMPHASIZE:
MENTAL AND THINKING

I RELY ON:
PERCEPTIONS AND LOGIC

CONFLICT TRIAD
HOW I DEAL WITH LOSS OR CHALLENGES

Positive

MY STYLE IS:
TO HELP OTHERS FEEL GOOD

I EMPHASIZE:
BEING UPLIFTING

I RELY ON:
BUILDING PEOPLE UP AND DENYING THERE IS A PROBLEM

INTERACTION TRIAD
HOW I GET WHAT I WANT FROM OTHERS

Against

MY STYLE IS:
TAKING ACTION, CREATING MOVEMENT, AND LEADING THE WAY

I EMPHASIZE:
BEING A STRONG PRESENCE

I RELY ON:
ACTIVELY TAKING CHARGE

Type 8 Collective
The Challenger or Active Controller

DESCRIPTION

MY VIBE IS
Powerful

8

"DESIRES TRUTH, FAIRNESS AND SITUATIONS TO BE UNDER CONTROL WHILE BEING BOLD AND PERCEIVING THINGS IN BLACK AND WHITE WITH NO GRAY AREA."

I WANT TO BE: **INVINCIBLE + FORCEFUL**
I RESIST BEING: **WEAK + COWARDLY**

AT MY BEST
"I am Competent"

OPEN UP TO OTHERS AND BE VULNERABLE
BE MORE CONCERNED ABOUT OTHERS WELL-BEING
EXPRESS SOFTER MORE GENTLE SIDES
BECOME MORE LOVING

Resourceful

8

Unresourceful

FEAR OTHERS WILL TURN ON THEM
BECOME DEFEATED OR DEPRESSED
BECOME LESS IN TOUCH WITH FEELINGS
WITHDRAW AND TAKE LESS ACTION IN THE WORLD

MOTIVATION

- TO HAVE CONTROL + JUSTICE
- TO BE PROTECTIVE

- TO AVOID FEELING VULNERABLE
- TO AVOID BEING WEAK

8

YOUR GIFT OR STRENGTH IS
Power

---

8 TALKING STYLE

Challenging

Big, Broad Statements

TYPICAL COMMENT: "I CAN HANDLE THIS."

WINGS

7 8 9

QUALITIES TO SUPPORT BEING INDEPENDENT
- IDEALISTIC
- ADVOCATING
- INSPIRING

QUALITIES TO SUPPORT BEING DIPLOMATIC
- CONFIDENT
- PATIENT
- PROTECTIVE

Use Both Wings

7 WING PARTICIPATING WITH LIGHTNESS AND FREEDOM
9 WING COMBINING STRENGTH WITH RECEPTIVITY

---

8 9 1
7   2
6 5 4 3

EXPRESSION TRIAD
HOW I KNOW BEST OR MAKE SENSE OF THINGS.

Body

MY STYLE IS:
TO BE PRODUCTIVE AND MAKE THINGS HAPPEN

I EMPHASIZE:
INSTINCT AND DOING

I RELY ON:
PHYSICAL SENSES AND BEING GROUNDED

CONFLICT TRIAD
HOW I DEAL WITH LOSS OR CHALLENGES

Reactive

MY STYLE IS:
FOCUSING ON FEELINGS AND ENERGY

I EMPHASIZE:
STRONG LIKES AND DISLIKES

I RELY ON:
LOOKING FOR AN EQUAL REACTION FROM OTHERS

INTERACTION TRIAD
HOW I GET WHAT I WANT FROM OTHERS

Against

MY STYLE IS:
TAKING ACTION, CREATING MOVEMENT, AND LEADING THE WAY

I EMPHASIZE:
BEING A STRONG PRESENCE

I RELY ON:
ACTIVELY TAKING CHARGE

MOTIVATION
- TO HAVE HARMONY • COMFORT
- TO FIND INNER STABILITY

- TO AVOID DIRECT CONFLICT
- TO AVOID OR PREVENT NEGATIVITY

9 YOUR GIFT OR STRENGTH IS *Harmony*

DESCRIPTION
MY VIBE IS
Peaceful
9 "DESIRES PEACE, HARMONY AND TO AVOID CONFLICT. DOESN'T READILY ACCESS OR EXPRESS THEIR OWN POINT OF VIEW. EMBRACES MULTIPLE PERSPECTIVES."

I WANT TO BE: EASY GOING • ACCEPTING
I RESIST BEING: PUSHY • AMBITIOUS

AT MY BEST
"*I am Comfortable*"

Resourceful/Unresourceful
BECOME MORE ENERGETIC • PRODUCTIVE
FEEL MORE SELF-CONFIDANT
LIVE LESS THROUGH OTHERS
TAKE MORE CONTROL OF LIFE

Resourceful
9
Unresourceful

BECOME SELF-DOUBTING • INDECISIVE
GET PASSIVE AND FALL INTO INACTIVITY
BECOME OVERWHELMED BY ANXIETY • WORRY
FEEL RIGID AND AWARE OF BEING UNREALISTIC

TALKING STYLE
9
Long Narrative
Saga

TYPICAL COMMENT: "EVERYTHING WILL BE OK."

WINGS
8 9 1

QUALITIES TO SUPPORT ADVISING
- SOCIAL
- SUPPORTIVE
- OBJECTIVE

QUALITIES TO SUPPORT NEGOTIATING
- FRIENDLY
- OPTIMISTIC
- ORDERLY

Use Both Wings
8 WING : BEING ASSERTIVE AND TAKING CHARGE
1 WING : CREATING STRUCTURE AND MOTIVATION

EXPRESSION TRIAD
HOW I KNOW BEST OR MAKE SENSE OF THINGS.
Body

MY STYLE IS:
TO BE PRODUCTIVE AND MAKE THINGS HAPPEN

I EMPHASIZE:
INSTINCT AND DOING

I RELY ON:
PHYSICAL SENSES AND BEING GROUNDED

CONFLICT TRIAD
HOW I DEAL WITH LOSS OR CHALLENGES
Positive

MY STYLE IS:
TO HELP OTHERS FEEL GOOD

I EMPHASIZE:
BEING UPLIFTING

I RELY ON:
BUILDING PEOPLE UP AND DENYING THERE IS A PROBLEM

INTERACTION TRIAD
HOW I GET WHAT I WANT FROM OTHERS
Away

MY STYLE IS:
TO PROCESS MY OWN THOUGHTS AND FEELINGS FIRST

I EMPHASIZE:
AN INWARD FOCUS OF MY ENERGY

I RELY ON:
MY INDEPENDENCE AND WITHDRAWING

Collectives Worksheets

REFER TO ALL NINE COLLECTIVES ON THE FOLLOWING WORKSHEETS.

Worksheets are on pages 59-66

Collectives Worksheet

What are you most attracted to and least attracted to about each type, and why?

TYPES

1

....

2

....

3

....

4

....

5

....

6

....

7

....

8

....

9

....

Collectives Worksheet

What are 1-2 qualities in each type that you see most in yourself?

TYPES

1

....

2

....

3

....

4

....

5

....

6

....

7

....

8

....

9

....

Collectives Worksheet

How would you describe the VIBE of this type as if
you were introducing a friend?

TYPES

1

....

2

....

3

....

4

....

5

....

6

....

7

....

8

....

9

....

Collectives Worksheet

How could you use the talking style of each type to have more options in your own communication?

TYPES

1

....

2

....

3

....

4

....

5

....

6

....

7

....

8

....

9

....

Collectives Worksheet

**How would the motivation of this type show you
how to understand this person's behavior better?**

TYPES

1

....

2

....

3

....

4

....

5

....

6

....

7

....

8

....

9

....

Collectives Worksheet

How would you support the type at their best? (*Resourceful*)
How would you support them at their worst? (*Unresourceful*)

TYPES

1

....

2

....

3

....

4

....

5

....

6

....

7

....

8

....

9

....

Collectives Worksheet

Select a "Triad Style" for each type, and consider how it might compliment your own style, or possibly challenge you somehow?

TYPES

1

....

2

....

3

....

4

....

5

....

6

....

7

....

8

....

9

....

Collectives Worksheet

What part of each type would you like to integrate
into yourself, and how would it serve you?

TYPES

1

....

2

....

3

....

4

....

5

....

6

....

7

....

8

....

9

....

Introducing
Enneagram Gifts

When each Enneagram type is at it's best,
wonderful gifts and personal strengths are naturally expressed.

EACH GIFT REPRESENTS A STRENGTH
YOU CAN USE OR DEVELOP.

UNWRAP YOUR GIFTS + STRENGTHS

The MOTIVATION cards contain the gifts + strengths.

How do your gifts + strengths help you?

- Increase your confidence.
- Express the greatest version of yourself.
- Become more of a gift to the people around you.

4 Steps

TO UNWRAP YOUR GIFTS + STRENGTHS

1 Learn

Learn the significance and purpose of each gift + strength.
By learning about each gift, the Enneagram becomes your tool for empowerment. See the GIFTS as as your source of confidence.

2 Explore

Explore how to receive each gift + strength.
To grow and transform we must embrace new qualities AND be willing to identify and release anything blocking those qualities.

3 Apply

Apply the gifts + strengths to your life/work/relationships.
The most important part of self-discovery is learning how your insights and new wisdom apply to your own personal life.

4 Action

Take the next step. Make an action plan.
Taking action is the final step to make it all matter. Only when you put your insight into action will you get results.

STEP 1

Learn

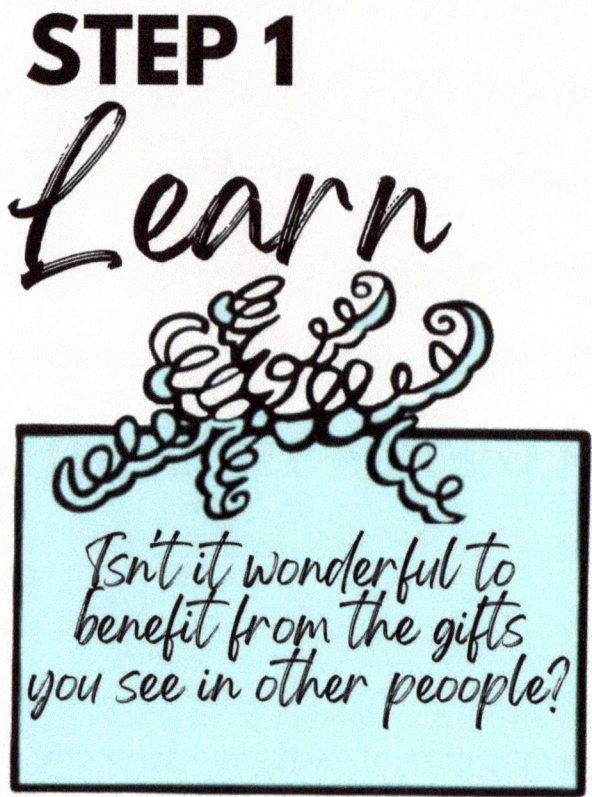

Isn't it wonderful to benefit from the gifts you see in other peoople?

You will relate with each gift + strength differently.

Your core type will likely be the easiest or most empowering gift to embrace.

Some gifts can be easy to receive, and some may feel challenging to find within yourself or to express. Each experience is part of your journey.

Give yourself permission to learn without judging or criticising yourself or your own process.

Learning is receiving.

You can not see a gift or strength in someone else without a deeper part of you knowing it is already within you.

STEP 1 - Learn the Gifts

1 Structure

Your gift at point one is an eye for details and refinement that makes regular stuff beautifully perfect.

It is easy for you to structure and organize everything into its best potential.

Your commitment to integrity is strong and mighty.

The gift of STRUCTURE provides a foundation for greatness.

2 Service

Your gift at point two is knowing how to make anyone feel great and cared for.

You can instantly read any room, group or gathering and know where to be a loving presence.

You can activate a positive emotional flow like no one else.

The gift of SERVICE is being generous and nurturing.

3 Radiance

Your gift at point three is seeing the goal, crushing the goal, then moving on to succeed at the next goal, all while being so efficient that it looks almost effortless to others.

Your ability to manifest and achieve (at mostly everything) inspires us all.

You are a radiant shining star who lights up the inner star within all of us.

The gift of RADIANCE is being a shining star inwardly and outwardly.

STEP 1 - Learn the Gifts

4

Your gift at point four is a deep heart that gives you the ability to see, feel, and express with meaning all things beautiful whether dark or light.

Your creative magic is like gold dust sprinkled on everything you touch.

You give us permission to FEEL all the things.

The gift of CREATIVITY brings beauty and depth to the world.

5

Your gift at point five is being objective and curious about everything.

Your way of being centered and present with what matters to you reflects a sturdy landing place that is within all of us.

Your wisdom and decision making ability is very impressive.

The gift of CURIOSITY offers wisdom and understanding.

6

Your gift at point six is being prepared and offering companionship and support to your people.

You have a natural guidance compass in your mind that gives everyone around you a sense of the right leadership and security.

You excel at being prepared, and you know what's going on at all times.

The gift of being PREPARED is supportive and brings safety and security.

STEP 1 - Learn the Gifts

7

Your gift at point seven is seeing the absolute best in all of us.

You believe that everything is possible, nothing is impossible, and moving forward is usually the best solution to everything.

Your enthusiasm is contagious to everyone around you.

The gift of ADVENTURE is making life joyful and free.

8

Your gift at point eight is making others feel protected and safe even in the most challenging situations.

You stand up for the underdog with fierce passion.

Your on-the-spot, black and white perspectives and directives are refreshing and empowering.

The gift of STRENGTH is being protective and powerful.

9

Your gift at point nine is seeing ALL perspectives with grace.

You are comfortable with views and ideas that are different from your own, and your energy brings harmony and peace.

When your own power emerges, it is a remarkable and harmonizing style of leadership.

The gift of HARMONY is being a comforting and spacious presence.

Worksheet
OWN YOUR GIFTS + STRENGTHS

- Choose your favorite quality in each gift + strength.
- Write it in the box to create your own chart of gifts. (Copy and Print!)
- Choose to express and share more of these gifts in your life.

STEP 2
Explore

Imagine the benefits of giving and receiving gifts with ease.

In this step we will explore two ways to connect with the gifts + strengths.

1: Growing toward them.

2: Letting go of what blocks them.

When you grow toward your gifts + strengths, you feel more empowered.

When you let go of blocks or limitations, you create space for something new.

This is the important inner work to prepare yourself to connect with all nine gifts of the Enneagram.

Living your best life includes being connected to your gifts + strengths.

Worksheet
EXPLORE THE GIFTS + STRENGTHS

GROW TOWARD

Structure 1

What do I need in order to do my best?

_____
_____
_____
_____

What is in the way of doing my best?

_____
_____
_____
_____

LET GO

Structure 1

GROW TOWARD

Service 2

What do I need to grow my nurturing side?

_____
_____
_____
_____

What is in the way of being in service?

_____
_____
_____

LET GO

Service 2

Worksheet
EXPLORE THE GIFTS + STRENGTHS

GROW TOWARD   What do I need to shine my own light?

Radiance 3

What is in the way of letting my light shine?   **LET GO**

Radiance 3

GROW TOWARD   What do I need to express my creativity?

Creativity 4

What is in the way of my creativity?   **LET GO**

Creativity 4

Worksheet

EXPLORE THE GIFTS + STRENGTHS

GROW TOWARD

What do I need to be curious?

(Curiosity — gift box, 5)

What is in the way of learning more?

LET GO

(Curiosity — gift box, 5)

GROW TOWARD

What do I need to prepare or to plan ahead?

(Prepared — gift box, 6)

What blocks me from being prepared?

LET GO

(Prepared — gift box, 6)

Worksheet

EXPLORE THE GIFTS + STRENGTHS

GROW TOWARD

What do I need to be more adventurous?

Adventure 7

What is in the way of being adventurous?

LET GO

Adventure 7

GROW TOWARD

What do I need to grow my inner strength?

Strength 8

What is in the way of being in my power?

LET GO

Strength 8

Worksheet

EXPLORE THE GIFTS + STRENGTHS

GROW TOWARD   What do I need to feel inner peace?

What is in the way of being in harmony?   **LET GO**

TIP: THE POWER OF RECEIVING

Receiving with confidence occurs when you understand that it benefits everyone involved.

If you want to be better at receiving, commit to practicing positive self-talk.

STEP 3

Apply

Growth happens when insights and learning are applied personally.

It's not enough to only grasp an idea; the crucial part is seeing how it relates to your own life.

To truly benefit from your insights and ideas, use your own experiences as the backdrop.

- To unlock new perspectives and opportunities, a powerful method is ASKING QUESTIONS.

- The worksheets feature tailored questions aimed at gaining strengths and empowerment through the gifts, and being able to improve any situation or challenge.

By posing the right questions, you can unveil fresh viewpoints and possibilities.

STEP 3 - Apply the Gifts
ASK YOURSELF SPECIFIC QUESTIONS

First, choose a current issue you want to work on. Write this issue at the top of the following worksheets to keep it top of mind. You will use ALL NINE GIFTS + STRENGTHS to handle your issue.

By consulting with the gifts + strengths, you find new perspectives and ways to handle your issue.

Questions to Consult each Gift + Strength

1) What is the right thing to do, and the right way to do it?
2) How can you improve on it?
3) What do you need to have in place?

1) What is most helpful?
2) Can you prioritize your own needs in order to offer more to others?
3) What do you need to extend more love?

1) What is the most productive option?
2) What is a more efficient approach?
3) What do you need shine your light?

1) What is your most authentic expression?
2) What is a more meaningful perspective?
3) What do you need to be creative or to find connection?

STEP 3 - Apply the Gifts

By consulting with all nine gifts + strengths, you gain a new approach to handle your issue.

Questions to Consult each Gift + Strength

1) What is your inner wisdom saying?
2) Can you understand more by being curious?
3) What would help you step back and observe?

1) What is the leadership or guidance needed?
2) Can you overcome fear by assessing worst case scenarios and planning for the best?
3) What do you need to feel safe and secure?

1) What would add fun and joyfulness here?
2) Can you focus on moving things forward?
3) What do you need ignite the enthusiasm?

1) What might need protection or action?
2) Can you take charge in another way?
3) What do you need to feel in control?

1) What comforting presence can you offer?
2) Can you be accommodating and see all sides objectively?
3) What do you need to establish harmony?

Example WORKSHEET

CHOOSE YOUR SPECIFIC ISSUE:

"SHOULD I MAKE A JOB CHANGE THAT MEANS LESS PAY BUT WOULD BE IN A FIELD I AM PASSIONATE ABOUT – OR – SHOULD I STAY WHERE I AM BECAUSE I'M COMFORTABLE AND GOOD AT MY CURRENT JOB?"

1 *Example* CONSULT WITH STRUCTURE

 What is the right thing to do and the right way to do it?
REMEMBER THAT I'M THE ONLY PERSON WHO KNOWS WHAT'S RIGHT FOR ME, REGARDLESS OF OTHER PEOPLE'S OPINIONS.

 How can you improve on it?
LAST YEAR I WANTED THIS CHANGE BUT TOLD MYSELF NO OUT OF FEAR.
I WOULD LIKE TO LET GO OF FEAR THIS TIME.

 What do you need to have in place?
I NEED TO BE CONFIDENT THAT I DESERVE TO DO WHAT MAKES ME FEEL GOOD.
I NEED TO WRITE MY GOALS AND USE A CALANDAR FOR INCOME PLANS.

2 *Example* CONSULT WITH SERVICE

 What is most helpful?
I THINK IT'S ME WHO WOULD BECOME MORE HELPFUL SINCE MY NEW JOB IS ABOUT HELPING OTHERS.

 Can you prioritize your own needs to offer more to others?
MY FAMILY WOULD BENEFIT FROM ME PRIORITIZING MY PASSION BECAUSE I WOULD BE INSPIRED, AND THEREFORE MORE INSPIRING TO BE AROUND.

 What do you need to extend more love?
I NEED TO LOVE THE PART OF ME THAT HAS WANTED THIS CHANGE FOR SO LONG INSTEAD OF ABANDONING IT.

Worksheet
APPLY THE GIFTS + STRENGTHS

THE ISSUE: (Use the same issue with all 9 gifts.)

1 CONSULT WITH STRUCTURE

 1) What is the RIGHT THING to do, and the right way to do it?

 2) How can you improve on it?

 3) What do you need in to have in place?

2 CONSULT WITH SERVICE

1) What is most helpful?

2) Can you prioritize your own needs in order to offer more to others?

3) What do you need to extend more love?

Worksheet

APPLY THE GIFTS + STRENGTHS

THE ISSUE: (Use the same issue with all 9 gifts.)

3 CONSULT WITH RADIANCE

 1) What is the most productive option?

 2) What is the most efficient approach?

 3) What do you need to shine your light?

4 CONSULT WITH CREATIVITY

 1) What is your most authentic expression?

 2) What another perspective you haven't imagined yet?

 3) Can you use some creative thinking or brainstorming?

Worksheet
APPLY THE GIFTS + STRENGTHS

THE ISSUE: (Use the same issue with all 9 gifts.)

5 CONSULT WITH CURIOSITY

✓ 1) What is your inner wisdom saying?

✓ 2) Can you understand more by being curious?

✓ 3) What would help you step back and observe with curiosity?

6 CONSULT WITH PREPAREDNESS

✓ 1) What is the leadership or guidance needed here?

✓ 2) Can you assess worst case scenarios and also prepare for the best?

✓ 3) What would help you feel safe, secure, and prepared?

Worksheet
APPLY THE GIFTS + STRENGTHS

THE ISSUE: (Use the same issue with all 9 gifts.)

7 CONSULT WITH ADVENTURE

✓ 1) What would add fun and joyfulness here?

✓ 2) Can you focus on moving things forward?

✓ 3) What would help you ignite positivity and enthusiasm?

8 CONSULT WITH STRENGTH

✓ 1) What is needing protection or action?

✓ 2) Can you take charge in another way?

✓ 3) What would help you feel in control?

Worksheet
APPLY THE GIFTS + STRENGTHS

THE ISSUE: (Use the same issue with all 9 gifts).

9 CONSULT WITH HARMONY

 1) What would be a comforting presence to offer?

 2) Can you see all sides objectively and peacefully?

 3) What would help you establish harmony?

Now you have nine new perspectives and nine new ways to apply your strengths!

The GIFTS + STRENGTHS are a map of treasures when you want to change or improve any situation you encounter.

STEP 4

Take Action

"Insight without action is just a daydream."

✓ You learned the significance of each gift + strength.

✓ You explored how to grow using the gifts + strengths.

✓ You applied new wisdom and insights to make it all matter. Now, the most important step is to TAKE ACTION.

In this step we will take the insights from step three and turn them into an ACTION plan.

Every step we take has the power to spark positivity and nudge us towards our dreams.

Action isn't just a stroll; it's a rocket ride to the growth, wisdom, and happiness you're going after.

Choose an action-minded journey to light up a dazzling tomorrow!

STEP 4 *Example*

✓ **Choose your best answer from each worksheet in STEP 3.**

✓ **Re-write your answer as action steps.**

You can do this for all 9 gifts, or a few , or just one if you prefer.

1 EXAMPLE - MY BEST ANSWER

✓ **What is the right thing to do?**
REMEMBER THAT I'M THE ONLY PERSON WHO KNOWS WHAT'S RIGHT FOR ME, REGARDLESS OF OTHER PEOPLE'S OPINIONS.

~~How can you improve on it?~~
~~LAST YEAR I WANTED THIS CHANGE BUT TOLD MYSELF NO OUT OF FEAR.~~
~~I WOULD LIKE TO LET GO OF FEAR THIS TIME.~~

~~What do you need in order to take your best action?~~
~~I NEED TO BE CONFIDENT THAT I DESERVE TO DO WHAT MAKES ME FEEL GOOD.~~

EXAMPLE ACTION STEPS

✓ MAKE A LIST OF MY OWN OPINIONS ABOUT THE NEW JOB.

✓ OUTLINE MY WINS IF I TAKE THE NEW JOB.

✓ SHARE MY CLEAR OPINIONS ABOUT MY BUDGET AND MAKE A PLAN FOR NEXT STEPS.

Worksheet
TAKE ACTION

MY BEST ANSWER:

MY ACTION STEPS:

 ✓

✓

MY BEST ANSWER:

MY ACTION STEPS:

 ✓

✓

Worksheet
TAKE ACTION

MY BEST ANSWER:

MY ACTION STEPS:

MY BEST ANSWER:

MY ACTION STEPS:

Worksheet
TAKE ACTION

MY BEST ANSWER:

MY ACTION STEPS: ✓

✓

MY BEST ANSWER:

MY ACTION STEPS: ✓

✓

Worksheet
TAKE ACTION

MY BEST ANSWER:

MY ACTION STEPS: ✓

✓

MY BEST ANSWER:

MY ACTION STEPS: ✓

✓

Worksheet
TAKE ACTION

MY BEST ANSWER:

MY ACTION STEPS: ✓

9 Harmony ✓

SUMMARY: CHOOSE YOUR TOP 3 ACTION STEPS

✓ _____

✓ _____

✓ _____

Strength Harmony Structure Service Radiance Creativity Curiosity Prepared Adventure

It's a Wrap!

- Use the gifts + strengths to handle your issues and challenges.
- Empower yourself and everyone around you.
- Access any gift or strength you need at any time.

AFFIRMATIONS

Custom Affirmations for each Enneagram Type

THE PURPOSE OF AFFIRMATIONS

to get support

when you want to grow

AFFIRM THE WISDOM OF YOUR TYPE

to get unstuck

when you need a positive mindset

for resilience

to build self-worth

Boost Your Life with FUNeagram™ Affirmations:

- Inspire the best version of yourself.
- Access qualities from other types to support your growth.
- Choose qualities to help you overcome challenges.
- Add qualities to build your positive mindset.
- Gain compassion and empathy by accessing other types.

Affirmations for Type 1

EMPOWERING QUALITIES

Principled

Objective

Structured

Straight-Forward

Integrity

I am principled in my actions and decisions.

I am highly organized in my life.

My structured nature allows me to excel.

I act with integrity and honesty.

I am committed to upholding my values and beliefs.

I embrace challenges as opportunities for growth.

I have unwavering faith in my abilities and talents.

I am forever evolving and improving.

Affirmations for Type 2

EMPOWERING QUALITIES

Warm

Giving

Generous

Interactive

Nurturing

My generosity is abundant.

My gift is being of service to the greater good.

I love to create connections with others.

My giving nature brings joy and happiness to others.

My nurturing spirit brings light to those in need of support.

I am warm and welcoming to everyone.

My loving energy creates goodness in the world.

My warmth and kindness create a positive environment.

Affirmations for Type 3

EMPOWERING QUALITIES

Driven

Adaptable

Ambitious

Competitive

Efficient

I am ambitious and driven.

I love being efficient.

As a natural competitor, I see challenges as opportunities.

I am adaptable and able to handle any situation.

I am comfortable being in the spotlight.

I am focused and determined with my goals.

I embrace change and use it to my advantage.

I am capable of achieving anything I set my mind to.

Affirmations for Type 4

EMPOWERING QUALITIES

Sensitive

Intense

Depth

Creative

Expressive

I am inspired to create beauty in the world.

My sensitivity is my strength.

I pursue my desires with intensity.

I explore my inner and outer world with curiosity and wonder.

Creativity and new ideas come naturally to me.

I seek meaningful connections to share my unique perspective.

I rely confidently in the wisdom of my heart and my feelings.

I value expressing my authentic self.

Affirmations for Type 5

EMPOWERING QUALITIES

Perceptive

Curious

Detached

Private

Inventive

My curiosity leads me to fascinating discoveries.

I am perceptive and notice details that others may miss.

I detach from the outcome, helping me offer objective support.

My privacy helps me focus on my personal growth.

I am constantly expanding my knowledge.

I am inventive and love to find solutions to problems.

I am open-minded, and willing to learn and grow.

My ability to practice detachment keeps me calm and centered.

Affirmations for Type 6

EMPOWERING QUALITIES

Devotion

Loyalty

Skeptical

Cautious

Prepared

I am a devoted friend and companion.

My skeptical thinking helps me make informed decisions.

Being cautious keeps me safe and helps me assess potential risks.

I am prepared for whatever comes my way.

My loyalty brings me deep fulfillment and happiness.

I trust my instincts to know where I need to go.

I let go of anxious thoughts to trust myself to handle things.

Following rules keeps me grounded and clear.

Affirmations for Type 7

EMPOWERING QUALITIES

Optimism

Adventure

Visionary

Spontaneous

Fun-loving

I am optimistic and excited to see what's next.

I am adventurous and open to new experiences.

I am visionary, capable of creating bright and exciting outcomes.

I am a fun-loving person who brings positivity to others.

I am confident in my ability to handle challenges.

I use my positive energy to bounce back quickly from setbacks.

I trust in love, happiness, abundance, and success.

My spontaneous mindset brings me joy.

Affirmations for Type 8

EMPOWERING QUALITIES

Protective

Independant

Assertive

Decisive

Powerful

I protect myself and others with compassion and strength.

I make decisions aligned with my values and goals.

I assert myself confidently and respectfully.

My strong intuition supports my decisiveness.

I am resilient and empowered in the face of adversity.

I set healthy boundaries and easily say "no" when needed.

I have the courage to stand up for myself and others.

I am worthy of respect and will not tolerate mistreatment from others.

Affirmations for Type 9

EMPOWERING QUALITIES

Agreeable

Spacious

Harmonious

Comfortable

Genuine

I create a spacious environment where others can feel valued.

My relationships are harmonious and understanding.

I accept myself and others without judgment or criticism.

I am genuine and authentic in my interactions.

I radiate positivity and attract positivity in return.

I give and receive love and compassion freely.

I trust in the wisdom of my deeper self.

My energy is relaxed and accepting.

Worksheets
USING AFFIRMATIONS

AFFIRMATION WORKSHEETS TO TRANSFORM YOUR LIFE

Worksheet #1 - Journaling

Worksheet #2 - Meditation

Worksheet #3 - Challenge Yourself

Worksheet #4 - Self Care

 Use FUNeagram™ affirmations to program your subconscious mind toward focusing on the good, and attracting more positivity into your life.

 FUNeagram™ affirmations are designed to learn and embrace your own Enneagram type, and help you connect with the other types as well.

 Note: FUNeagram™ affirmations resonate with the motivations and the positive qualities of each Enneagram type.

Worksheet
AFFIRMATIONS
FOR JOURNALING

- Choose two affirmations, and answer the prompts for each.
  Prompt #1: Why does this matter to me at this time?
  Prompt #2: How do I feel when this is true for me?

Affirmation #1

Affirmation #2

Why does it matter?

Why does it matter?

How do I feel when it's true for me?

How do I feel when it's true for me?

Worksheet
USING AFFIRMATIONS FOR MEDITATION

- Choose one affirmation about something you want.
- Meditate on this affirmation. Focus on the INTELLIGENCE STYLES to tap into your different styles of intelligence (Body, Heart, and Head) while repeating the affirmation to yourself.

BODY STYLE: What's your intuition telling you about it?
HEART STYLE: What are your feelings telling you about it?
HEAD STYLE: What do you think or believe about it?

- Notice the different ways you experience the affirmation in your Body, Heart, and Head.

One Affirmation I want right now:

Do you have a different connection to the affirmation within your Body, Heart, and Head?

Worksheet
USING AFFIRMATIONS
TO CHALLENGE YOURSELF

- Choose an affirmation you resist or doubt, even if just a little.
- Look for ways to overcome your resistance and doubt.
- Challenge yourself to see a new truth for yourself.

One Affirmation I resist or doubt:

What's a better way to say it (to erase your doubts)?

How are my resistance and doubts holding me back?

Insights about my resistance and doubts:

Worksheet

USING AFFIRMATIONS FOR SELF CARE

- Choose an "Affirmation for Today."
- How does it support your overall self care?
- What do you notice about your self-talk?

Today's Affirmation

What do I notice about my self talk working with this Affirmation?

MORE WAYS TO USE
The FUNeagram™

HELP OTHERS
FIND THEIR TYPE

FUNeagram™ workbooks and cards are a useful resource for coaches, teachers, therapists, and organizations using the Enneagram.

TEACHING, GROUP COACHING,
LEADERSHIP PROGRAMS

Make learning the Enneagram easier and accessible! A great tool for groups, workshops, presentations, or events. Book sessions or events via the website.

IMPROVE
RELATIONSHIPS

FUNeagram™ offers new perspectives and resources for couples, business relationships, and small groups to increase understanding and deepen compassion and connection.

RESOURCES FOR
LEARNING

We offer resources for anyone who works with the Enneagram in any setting. Inquire through the website, or visit the shop.

Resources

LEARN THE ENNEAGRAM THE F-U-N WAY

 **FIND YOUR TYPE**    **UNDERSTAND YOURSELF**    **NEXT STEPS FOR GROWTH**

Free Bonus

ILLUSTRATED MINI-POSTER
Visualize the Enneagram

 Email jen@funeagram.com saying *"I Want the Poster"* to receive a file you can print in any size.

IN THE SHOP

PRINTED CARD DECKS

JOURNALS

AFFIRMATION CARDS

DIGITAL CARDS

DIGITAL WORKBOOKS

DONE-FOR-YOU WORKSHOP KITS

BUNDLES FOR EACH TYPE

FUNeagram.com

STILL EXPLORING?

If you don't have the feeling of clarity you desire, let us know if we can help you continue exploring.

We want to keep your Enneagram journey FUN!

We offer coaching sessions and typing interviews to help you reach personal goals through the Enneagram.

Resources

Check out our list of books, podcasts, articles, and online tests to support your Enneagram journey.
Go to the website: www.FUNeagram.com

We're always updating the list, so if you have a favorite resource, please forward it to us!

Connect with Us

Follow us on Instagram @funeagram

Join the Facebook Group. (Search FUNeagram on Facebook)

Sign up for our newsletter on the website.
(and check out the free stuff!)

Email: jen@funeagram.com

XXOO
Jen & Team Fun

FUNEAGRAM.COM

FULL DISCLAIMER posted on website. For Informational purposes only.

Jenifer Novak

Professional Coach, Certified Enneagram Teacher, Author, Speaker

Jenifer has worked in the field of personal growth for 20 years. She specializes in teaching and coaching people to use inner resources for empowerment, and to connect with their creativity and authenticity.

She has certifications in professional coaching through JFK University and The Ford Institute, Spiritual Coaching through The Chopra Center, Enneagram Accreditation through The Integrative Enneagram, and a BA in Fine Art.

She is the creator of FUNeagram™ cards, workbooks, children's books, journals and coaching programs.

How the Enneagram Changes Lives

"It helped me feel like I'm normal and not alone! We are who we are, AND we can always improve ourselves. I needed to find a balance of growing and accepting myself at the same time."

"I have much more compassion and patience for myself, and definitely with others in my life. Now I know what direction to take on my healing journey."

"It gave me insight into my unhealthy choices. It also validated my desires such as love, belonging, being appreciated and having good relationships. I feel stronger about going after my goals because of knowing why I want certain things."

"It has given me the chance to understand who I am, and shift to a place where I do not hold my type against me. I see myself through every number in given situations, which is how I have grown the most from the Enneagram."

*Edited from a survey conducted in our Facebook group.

Reflecting on your F-U-N journey.

F *What have you discovered about your Enneagram type?*

U *How do you see yourself and others differently?*

N *What steps are you planning to take toward growth?*

**To love oneself
is the beginning of
a life long romance.**

Oscar Wilde

Testimonials

We highly value using the Enneagram in our therapy practice to help clients gain deeper self-understanding. However, teaching it during sessions has always been a challenge! Discovering FUNeagram was a delightful game-changer. **The Enneagram's benefits have become much more accessible and user-friendly.** All of our therapists find it easier to teach and report improvements in their own skills and personal growth.

-Jalena Rusaw, LMFT Horizon Counseling Center

My team of Technology Consultants attended a FUNeagram Workshop to learn business growth through the Enneagram. None of us were familiar with the Enneagram, and **the FUNeagram approach made it easy to understand each other and how we can work together more effectively as a team.**

-Karl W. Palachuk, Author, Coach, Small Biz Thoughts Technology Community

I'm amazed how quickly I was able to find my type and easily understand how the Enneagram works. **This is a great "quick reference" when I need a better perspective dealing with others.** Learning step-by-step is such an accelerated and FUN way to grow. I'm sharing the FUNeagram with my team at work, and it's also a great gift for my clients.

-Marsha Solk Beer, Realtor

Testimonials

This workbook is a fantastic guide that I will turn to time and again to access wisdom and to move toward awareness and compassion for myself and my clients!

-Debbie Leoni, MCC, Certified Enneagram Practitioner

FUNeagram is one of the greatest and most creative resources to come out of the Enneagram world!

-Sue Ryan, TEDx, Speaker, Author, Leadership Coach

When I learned the DESCRIPTIONS and then matched them with the MOTIVATIONS **I had a breakthrough with two members on my team at work!** I couldn't make sense of WHY we got stuck making group decisions until I could finally release my negative judgement of their behaviors. Now I can see how their types actually contribute to better decisions. This is a great quick-reference tool I keep permanently in my desk!

Joanna Daley, Sales

The FUNeagram helped me see beyond my self-imposed limitations! I'm able to achieve extreme clarity with how to be more effective in my work. It's helping me get out of my own way as I grow my business.

-Stephanie Chandler, CEO, Authority Publishing

Notes

Notes

Notes